T0094111

Workflow

A Practical Guide to the Creative Process

Workflow

A Practical Guide to the Creative Process

Doron Mayer

CRC Press
Taylor & Francis Group
Boca Raton London New York

CRC Press is an imprint of the
Taylor & Francis Group, an **informa** business

CRC Press
Taylor & Francis Group
6000 Broken Sound Parkway NW, Suite 300
Boca Raton, FL 33487-2742

© 2018 by Taylor & Francis Group, LLC
CRC Press is an imprint of Taylor & Francis Group, an Informa business

International Standard Book Number-13: 978-1-138-05853-8 (paperback); 978-1-138-05855-2 (hardback)

Library of Congress Cataloging-in-Publication Data

Names: Mayer, Doron, author.
Title: Workflow : a practical guide to the creative process / Doron Mayer.
Description: Boca Raton, FL : CRC Press, Taylor & Francis Group, 2018.
Identifiers: LCCN 2017034657| ISBN 9781138058538 (pbk. : alk. paper) | ISBN 9781138058552 (hardback : alk. paper)
Subjects: LCSH: Work. | Creative ability.
Classification: LCC BF481 .M392 2018 | DDC 153.3/5--dc23
LC record available at https://lccn.loc.gov/2017034657

Visit the eResources:
http://www.crcpress.com/product/isbn/9781138058538

Visit the Taylor & Francis Web site at
http://www.taylorandfrancis.com

and the CRC Press Web site at
http://www.crcpress.com

To Dad, who inspired me to create.
To Mom, who inspired me to teach.

Contents

SECTION III The Concept: From a Blank Page to An Exciting Core Idea 45

SECTION IV The Vision: From Raw Concept to Solid Vision 81

SECTION VIII   **The Principles: A Deeper Look at the Fundamentals of the Creative Workflow**   **255**

Preface

Dear reader,

We all start life as creatives. As kids, we are fascinated with making stuff, and we have an imagination that knows no boundaries. Some of us lose interest early on; others continue to create as a hobby their entire lives; and some of us make it our career.

We quickly discover that professional creativity comes with a sting. It is no longer the relaxing pastime it once was. Creativity is a wild creature, and it doesn't like it when you try to harness it with plans and deadlines. Frustration and pain often dominate the first few years in one's creative career.

I remember a conversation, about three years into my career as an animator, in which I shared my difficulty with my then-supervisor. "With every task I get," I told him, "I feel like I've been tossed into rough water and I need to get to the other side—except, I don't know how to swim. I kick and flail around, gulping water, coughing, struggling to stay afloat—and somehow, in most cases, I make it; but then

I'm completely exhausted. It's an unpleasant experience. How do I learn to swim? How do I work in a more controlled way?"

My supervisor's answer was, "you'd better get used to it because that's just the way it is."

* * *

Years later, I was animating on *Asterix and the Vikings*—my first feature film. The quality demanded was higher than anything I had experienced before, and although I worked hard, I was never happy with my animation. I knew I could do better, and I knew what I wanted to achieve, but somehow, I just couldn't make it happen.

While that was going on, I happened to pick up a small book about screenwriting called *How to Write for Animation*, by Jeffrey Scott. Interestingly, it said almost nothing about what a good script should be like. Instead, it focused on the practical process of writing. "Start here, then do this, but be careful not to do that"—that's the kind of advice the book was full of.

As I was reading, it struck me that many of these process tips may also be applicable in animation. Replace a few writing terms with animation terms, and you get something you can use. I started applying these tips in my work, and amazingly, it turned out to be just the kind of advice I needed. Not only did it help me overcome my anxieties, but it also improved my actual animation!

That experience left a deep and long-lasting impression on me. A book about *writing* helped me become a better *animator*; what did that mean? Would it also be helpful in other creative fields? Could there be an approach that would work for *every* kind of creative field?

I had to figure it out. Over the next decade or so, I spent a lot of time studying the creative process in different art forms. I looked into writing, web design, painting, architecture, music, game design, sculpting, and of course, animation. I also tried to be constantly aware of my own process. Which strategies proved consistently helpful? What were the common pitfalls?

Gradually, a set of methods emerged: a robust workflow that brings about a sense of control, while embracing the inhenrently chaotic nature of creativity. I started implementing these methods—not only in my own work but also in managing creative teams, directing large projects, teaching students, and coaching fellow artists. Over and over again, the workflow proved to be helpful.

This book is my answer to the question I asked my supervisor at the beginning of my career. It is the book I would have loved to have read back then; it would have saved me years of pain and frustration. Whatever creative field you're in, I hope these ideas will help you work with confidence and flow—and most importantly, enjoy the process.

Doron Mayer

Acknowledgments

This book would not have been possible without the help and support of many good people, who have invested their valuable time in helping me see it to fruition.

First and foremost, I'd like to thank my sister, Keren, who played a key role in helping me simplify the book's structure and focus my efforts on what really matters.

A huge thank you to my better half, Eline Rozen, whose support of this long journey never waned, whose capacity for listening to my blabbering about it seemed endless, and who has, willingly and without complaint, endured the many months of me spending more time with the computer than with her.

Thanks also to the many people who have granted me their moral support and constructive feedback over the years. In that regard, a special thank you goes to Michelle Orrelle, Kfir Ram, and Tal Lotan.

Thank you to Sean Connelly and the team at CRC press, who, in the process of realizing this book, have done their best to accommodate my every request.

Thank you to the prolific Rafi Ben Aharon (Byron), who generously allowed me to use his artwork and creative process for examples in areas I am not proficient in.

Heartfelt thanks to the greatest teacher I ever had or will have, the late Oswald Adler, who showed me the connection between art and logical thinking.

Finally, a huge thank you and a hug to the thousands of creators who share their creative process online, bravely exposing their mistakes, uncertainties, and private working methods. This book is as much from you as it is for you.

Author

Doron Mayer (Meir) has been working as a professional creator for more than 20 years. His areas of practice include writing, animation, storyboarding, design, and illustration. He worked on films (*The Secret Life of Pets*), television series (*Shaun the Sheep*), and computer games (*Hitman*). He also created mobile applications, illustrated children's books, sculpted, and wrote music. Doron has supervised teams of 30 artists and more, taught hundreds of students and delivered dozens of lectures and seminars.

His varied career has been made possible through a set of universal creativity methods that he has been developing for over a decade.

Introduction

The Bucket and the Pipeline

Imagine your talent, your raw artistic skills, your professional knowledge—in short, everything you know and are capable of doing—as a bucket of water. The fuller your bucket, the higher the quality you're able to achieve. Right?

Well, not exactly.

For simple creative work that takes a couple of hours, yes: your talent and craftsmanship are all that matters. For longer projects, however, there's more to it than that. When a project takes days, weeks, or even months to complete (perhaps with some teamwork involved), you don't get to pour your "bucket" directly into the final work. Instead—if I may stretch this metaphor just a little further—your skill and talent need to flow through many different junctions, considerations, and obstacles into a final work that lies quite far in the future. The amount of water in your bucket is no longer the only thing that matters: the quality of your *pipeline* is at least as important. If your pipeline is full of holes and dead-ends, and your project is long and complex, you can start with a huge bucket of talent and skill and passion and end up with just a few drops of quality at the other end (Figure 0.1).

FIGURE 0.1   *Artists tend to focus on filling their buckets with talent, raw skill and knowledge, but if the pipeline is full of holes and dead-ends, only a few drops of it will make it through to the final work.*

Unfortunately, many of us aren't fully aware of the workflow as an issue. Looking to improve our work—or when things go wrong—we tend to put all our resources in improving our raw skill: we buy books, take expensive professional courses, watch tutorials, and practice. When we keep bumping into the same kind of problems, we do more of the same, not realizing it's not our raw skills that we need to upgrade. It's our *workflow*.

So, how do you go about upgrading your workflow?

I have good news: you're already well on your way. Just by picking up this book and reading these first few pages, you have effectively told your brain that your workflow *is* important. As long as you keep that awareness, your brain will notice and process workflow-related information. It might take you a while, but inevitably, you *are* going to get better at it. The rest of the book is just a shortcut.

In the following pages, I'll do my best to get you there faster with a set of methods I have found to be consistently and almost universally effective (Figure 0.2).

FIGURE 0.2   *A great creative workflow will help you realize the full potential of your raw talent, passion, and skill.*

Chaos and Control

The idea of a "universal creative workflow" can be surprisingly controversial. People don't like to think of creativity as something that can be systemized. They often say that creativity is "individual," "uncontrollable," and "unpredictable."

They are not entirely wrong, but also not entirely right.

It's true that you can't manage the creative process the same way you mange many other human activities. Chaos and uncertainly are necessary components of the workflow, as we shall see going forward. But even though you may not be able to control it in the simple sense of the word, with the right set of methods, you *can* get it to flow to where you need it to go.

It is also true that the creative process is an individual thing. But once you're prepared to look past the myth of creativity, it's actually possible to notice strategies that work for *most* people *most* of the time, as well as strategies that consistently *don't* work. In this book, we will take a good look at both types.

Ultimately, it will be your job to try out these strategies and make them your own. Take what works for you, modify what doesn't, and add your own strategies to the mix. Soon, you'll have a creative workflow that's tailored to your personal creative ways, and that allows every drop in your bucket of talent and passion and skill to travel all the way to your final work.

How to Use This Book

The book is arranged in eight sections.

Section I is a quick overview of the five elements of the creative workflow. It explains briefly the role of each element in the process and gives you a sense of how they function together.

In *Sections II–VI*, we'll delve into each element separately. I'll show you some effective strategies and explain how and why they work. I'll also share a few "safety rules"—strategies that *don't* work as well and should be avoided.

Section VII is a complete demonstration of the workflow, starting from scratch and ending with a refined piece. This case study touches on most of the strategies and tips discussed in this book and allows you to see them in action.

In *Section VIII* we'll tie it all together again with a second and deeper overview. Now that you're familiar with the workings of each element separately, this section will give you a clearer view of *why* the workflow works the way it does.

Reading the Book

The creative workflow is not an easy thing to explain, nor is it an easy one to get your head around at first. A lot of the tips and approaches are intertwined: to understand A, you need to understand B, but to understand B, you need to understand A. I have done my best to disentangle those knots, but ultimately, it may take a few reading passes to fully grasp everything in these pages.

I suggest that you start with a light read-through, front to back. The book will take you through a logical step-by-step learning experience. During that first read, try to skim over difficult parts and focus on just taking the whole thing in.

Then, give the book a second read. This time, slow down and spend some time on challenging spots. The interdependency of concepts, previously an obstacle, will now come to your aid: understanding *some* of the concepts will help you understand the rest of them. You can expect to gain a much better understanding of the creative workflow once you've gone through the book a second time.

As you continue to work, create and grow, I suggest you give the book a quick read every once in a while. Strategies and concepts will continue to fall into place and become clearer as you get more and more used to working with them.

The Book as a Reference Guide

In time, you may want to refresh your memory on a specific topic, rather than the workflow as a whole. To help you get to the information you need quickly, the book offers the following tools:

Color coding. Each of the five elements of the creative workflow has its own color. Use the colored strip to get to the section you need quickly.

Printable summaries. At the end of each section, you'll find a single-page summary of the most important ideas and advice in that section. Those summary pages can be photocopied or downloaded and printed from the book's website.

Glossary. The glossary is a great way to refresh your memory on key concepts without having to reread the entire book. For ease of reference, it is also color coded per element.

Website. The book's website contains additional examples that could not be included in the book, downloadable summaries, and more. Be sure to check it out at https://www.crcpress.com/9781138058538 and http://theworkflowbook.com/.

A Note about Language

In writing about the creative workflow as a standalone skill, *language* has been my greatest challenge. The existing workflow lingo is hopelessly intermingled with field-specific lingo. The same workflow method will often have different names in different fields, whereas some methods don't have a name at all. I believe this language barrier is part of the reason people find it hard to think of the process as a standalone skill. We tend to think with the language we have.

Writing this book required, therefore, the creation of a completely new *workflow lingo*. In most cases, I have adopted existing terms, but in some cases, I've had to get quite creative with it. For one central workflow concept, I even had to come up with a completely new word.

While the book offers plenty of practical workflow tips, perhaps the more important thing it provides you with is a standalone workflow lingo. With that new lingo, you can continue to think about your workflow, analyze it, talk about it with you peers, and improve on it.

What to Expect

With your new workflow tools and language, what kind of results can you expect to see in your work?

Confidence. The methods in this book are designed to reduce anxiety and confusion and replace them with focus and clarity. You can expect an almost immediate effect on your creative confidence.

Dissolve creative blocks. The book is full of tips that'll help you avoid creative blocks and, in those rare cases they do occur, get around them quickly.

Structured chaos. You'll learn how to control your work without compromising the much-needed chaos of creative thinking.

Flexibility and growth. Because this is about the process as a standalone skill, you'll be able to use these methods across many different creative fields. That means you'll be able to expand your abilities quickly. This is particularly good for freelancing: you'll find it easier to evolve with the market, making more options and opportunities available to you. It's also great for working in small studios and indie productions, where interdisciplinary flexibility is required and appreciated.

Collaboration across teams. Understanding the process as a standalone skill will help you understand the needs of other departments and teams, and collaborate with them. This is great for creatives who work in larger productions, involving many separate and specialized teams.

Leadership. If you're leading a team, a deep understanding of the creative workflow will help you understand and support your crew. If you're not in a leadership role yet, understanding the workflow on that level will help you get there.

Originality. The workflow is going to help you put more of yourself into your work, so that it stands out as fresh and unique.

Flow. Does your work feel too labored at times? A good workflow can make it feel simpler, smoother, and more effortless.

Structural and conceptual clarity. Your work will be easier for your audience to follow and understand. Whether it's an intellectual message or just pure emotional impact, the audience will never miss it or be confused about what it is you're trying to convey.

Refinement. You'll learn a set of methods that'll allow you to refine and enrich your work with texture and details without losing focus or feeling overwhelmed.

All this may sound a bit overreaching. Can it really be achieved just by improving your workflow, without learning anything new about your specific creative field?

To that, my answer is an unflinching YES. I hope that by finish reading this book, you'll think so too.

THE FIVE ELEMENTS

The Creative Workflow
at a Glance

"If you give a good idea to a mediocre team, they will screw it up. If you give a mediocre idea to a brilliant team, they will either fix it or throw it away and come up with something better."

Ed Catmull

In this short first section, I'd like to give you a quick overview of the five elements of the creative workflow: Capture, Concept, Vision, Production, and Plan.

| CAPTURE | CONCEPT | VISION | PRODUCTION | PLAN |

I'll explain the role of each element in the workflow and how they all work together. This should help keep you oriented as we later delve deep into each element in turn.

Let's begin with the middle three: Concept, Vision, and Production.

The Concept-Vision-Production Workflow

| CAPTURE | CONCEPT | VISION | PRODUCTION | PLAN |

Concept, Vision, and Production are the three stages a typical creative project goes through. Notice how each stage requires a different mindset:

The Concept. This is the first stage, in which you come up with an exciting *concept* for the work. It's a carefree, playful, and unpredictable stage, in which you jump from this to that, fool around, get easily excited—and then, just as easily, disconnect and try something else. We'll talk about Concept in Section III.

The Vision. In this stage, you develop your concept into a full creative *vision*. This is a slower, more intellectual stage, in which you get curios and geek out about your subject matter. You learn about it, practice it, test it, and take notes of everything you discover. We'll discuss the Vision in Section IV.

The Production. This stage, which is the longest of the three, is where you forge your actual work. Here, you get practical and follow the plan. You still need to improvise and think creatively, but your main focus is on doing the job on time, while getting as close as possible to your creative vision. We'll look into the Production process in Section V.

I like to think of these three stages—the playful, the intellectual, and the practical—as having my own inner creative dream team.

At each stage, I "step into character" and adopt the appropriate mindset for the task at hand; once I've completed the stage, I "hand it over" to the next person. Although a bit oversimplified, I find this idea helpful in understanding and managing the creative process.

In my analysis of the workflow, I have come to realize that much of the struggle and frustration creatives experience on a daily basis comes from those three inner personas fighting between themselves for control. When your volatile Concept persona starts coming up with new and exciting ideas while you're trying to produce something, that can be destructive to your workflow. When the scholarly Vision persona starts solving problems in the middle of a playful brainstorming session, that too is not helpful.

Many of the struggles and frustrations creatives experience in their work come from their inner personas fighting for control.

So, here's my first practical workflow tip: keep those three stages separate and well defined. In other words: make sure that at any given point in the process, you know exactly which inner persona you're supposed to be working with and that no other persona is allowed to interfere. This one simple change can go a long way in reducing creative anxiety. We'll talk more about how to do this in future sections.

The Plan

CAPTURE	CONCEPT	VISION	PRODUCTION	PLAN

Every team needs a manager to run smoothly, and your inner dream team is no exception. The fourth persona you'll need to adopt is therefore the *manager*.

Managing is not a stage in the process; it's a role you'll assume whenever needed—usually a few times a day—throughout the project.

As the manager, you're at the control tower. You see the big picture and plan what to do when. You keep track of things, and make sure your inner team is collaborating effectively. You also make sure the work keeps within the framework of deadlines, client requests, and your own resources.

The Capture

CAPTURE	CONCEPT	VISION	PRODUCTION	PLAN

The fifth element of the workflow—which is really the first—is not another persona but a *skill*: the ability to quickly and clearly *capture* the essence of an idea. As we shall see, this seemingly simple skill is the basic building block of the creative workflow—the one skill that makes it all possible. That makes it the perfect place to begin our journey.

THE CAPTURE

The Building Block of the Creative Workflow

"I have made this letter longer because I have not had time to make it shorter."

Blaise Pascal

Chapter 1

A Superskill

Suppose I asked you to write a description of the image in Figure 1.1 in such a way that someone reading it would be able to reconstruct the image with reasonable accuracy in his or her imagination. How would you go about doing that?

Well, you'll probably write down everything you notice about this image. You'd write about the colors, the composition, the shape of the house, and the naked trees in the background. You'll describe details, like the pieces of wood on the roof and the crude stones that support the structure. The task may be tedious, but it's simple enough—at least, in the sense that it doesn't require a high level of skill. Most people would be able to do it reasonably well.

FIGURE 1.1 *How would you describe this image to someone who has never seen it?*

What if I asked you to do the same thing in only 40 words?

This is an entirely different kind of challenge. How do you squeeze everything you see in this image into just 40 words? What do you include? What do you omit?

Let's try it now. Grab something to write with and a sheet of paper, and let's do this exercise together. Your goal is to write a description in 40 words (or fewer) that would allow a person who has never seen the original photo to imagine something that's as close to it as possible.

Ready? Go.

* * *

Welcome back. How did it go?

The following is the description I came up with. Let me stress that I am *not* showing you the "right" way of doing it—there are no correct or incorrect answers here. I'm just sharing it with you because I think it would be interesting to compare the results:

> *Medieval country house in autumn. White walls hang on crooked timber frame, like pale skin over an old man's skeleton. Naked branches droop over straw beaver-brown roof. A patch of strikingly green grass stands against the overall gloom.*

What we just did—each in his or her own way—was to *capture* what we see as the most essential aspects of the image.

I used a written description for this exercise because it's a medium everybody knows how to use, but capturing doesn't have to be done with words necessarily. For example, I could capture the image with paint (Figure 1.2).

FIGURE 1.2   *Capturing the essence of the image with paint.*

It can also be captured with clay, 3D modeling, or any other creative medium—even music (although that, of course, would be

CAPTURE | CONCEPT | VISION | PRODUCTION | PLAN |

a more abstract kind of capture). The subject doesn't have to be visual, either. You can capture an idea, an experience, a design concept, or even just a feeling.

To summarize: *a capture* is simply a description that is at once as brief as possible and as clear as possible. You're basically taking a complex and detailed subject and squeezing it into a compressed capsule of information. You can then give that capsule to an audience, and they should be able to reconstruct the original subject in their minds. The better you are at capturing, the more accurate their reconstruction would be (Figure 1.3).

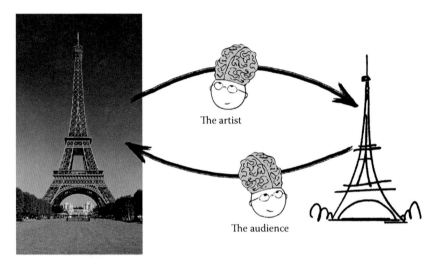

The artist

The audience

FIGURE 1.3   Capturing squeezes a complex subject into a compressed capsule of information.

Why Is This Important?

Capturing sounds like a nice skill to have, but why should it be *that* important?

Here are four reasons capturing is absolutely essential to your workflow.

Communication. Capturing allows you to show an idea to someone—and discuss it—long before you've actually created it. You simply squeeze the idea into that compressed form, present it to the other person, and—if you've done a good job capturing—he or she would be able to get a clear view of what's locked inside your brain.

Focus. The subject you're describing probably includes many details and attributes. Some are central to what you want to express, others—not so much. By forcing you to choose a specific point of view and identify what's essential to it, the act of capturing creates focus. Take a look at my two captures of the old house earlier: in both mediums (text and paint), I have included only those details that I perceived to be essential to the theme.

Experimenting. The better you are at capturing your ideas with both speed and clarity, the easier it is for you to experiment with different options. As we'll see, these quick throwaway captures play an important part in both the Concept stage and the Vision stage of the workflow.

Refinement. A detailed piece that takes a long time to refine doesn't happen linearly from A to Z. Instead, you start with a crude version of the entire work and then gradually layer in the details, from major to minor. Each layer is called a *pass*, and with every pass, you add in only the most vital details for that specific pass. In other words, every pass is a really a *capture*, and a polished work is achieved by layering those captures, one on top of the other.

If that last part left you somewhat confused, that's okay. Section V is entirely dedicated to the idea of working in passes. The only reason I brought it up here is to let you know that capturing isn't just a planning and experimenting tool. It also has a crucial role in forging your final work. I find it beautiful that the very skill that allows us to scribble a quick note or a rough doodle is also the skill that allows us to create slow, detailed, highly polished artwork.

I hope you're beginning to see how the seemingly unremarkable skill of capturing is in fact an important part of the creative process. It sharpens your perception, improves your ability to collaborate, and is used extensively in all three stages of the work (Concept, Vision and Production).

Like all skills, capturing comes naturally to some, less naturally to others. The good news is that you can get better at it. All you need is a bit of practice—and a handful of practical capturing techniques.

CAPTURE

CONCEPT | VISION | PRODUCTION | PLAN |

Chapter 2

Capturing Techniques

Get Personal

In the capture exercise of the old Danish country house, how different was your description from what I had suggested?

Probably quite different. That doesn't mean one of us was wrong, of course. The reason we came up with different descriptions is that we each had to *choose* the most important aspects of the subject, and choice is always a matter of personal view.

To illustrate: which one of the sketches in Figure 2.1 *accurately* depicts the Eiffel Tower?

The answer, of course, is that none of them do. They all depict a *subjective* interpretation. If you think of the Eiffel Tower as an elegant, streamlined thing, your capture might look like sketch A. If you think it's a heavy, black, iron thing that reminds you of the industrial era, you might do something like sketch B. Or, if you see the tower as a cheerful thing that symbolizes the jaunty Parisian atmosphere, maybe you'll capture it as sketch C.

CAPTURE | CONCEPT | VISION | PRODUCTION | PLAN |

FIGURE 2.1   *Which is the real Eiffel Tower?*

None of these are objective, yet most people will instantly recognize all of them as the Eiffel Tower. More importantly, they will be able to see the Eiffel Tower through the eyes—or more accurately, through the *mind*—of the artist who made the sketch.

I used the drawing medium in this example, but the same thing can be done with any other medium—for example, words. Consider the following descriptions:

    A. *The dark arches of the Eiffel Tower loomed over my head.*

    B. *The inexplicable tangle that is the Eiffel Tower swirled joyfully over my head.*

Do you see how this works the same way? By allowing yourself the freedom to abandon objectivity and get personal, you can choose the lens through which your audience sees your subject.

Wet Captures

A great way of getting more expressive with your captures is to ask yourself questions about the subject as a *whole*. Try to keep your questions highly subjective: what does the subject *mean* to me? How do I *feel* about it? What does it *remind* me of?

These questions produce insightful and expressive captures that are based on metaphors, intuition, free association, and common human values. I call those *wet captures* because they're juicy and abstract. We've already seen how it works with the Eiffel Tower example: "It *feels* elegant and streamlined," "It *reminds me* of the industrial era," and "It *symbolizes* the Parisian atmosphere."

Let's look at another wet capture. Consider the two drawings in Figure 2.2 (from one of my scenes in *Asterix and the Vikings*). Although they look simple enough, these drawings can take a while to draw. Suppose I wanted to show my animation supervisor what I had in mind for those two poses before I took the time to actually draw them. How would I go about it?

With wet captures, this can be done in seconds: all I need to do is capture the essence of each pose as a whole. Basic as they are, these two captures are going to give my supervisor a good idea of what the scene is going to feel like once animated.

FIGURE 2.2 *Wet capturing is about how the subject makes you **feel**. In this case: pose A feels closed and contracted. It reminds me of a knot. Pose B is the exact opposite: It feels open and stretched out, and it reminds me of a happy splash of water. These impressions can be wet-captured very quickly, with just a few lines.*

Dry Captures

Dry captures represent the opposite approach: instead of capturing it as a whole, you simplify your subject by taking it apart. Figure 2.3 shows what a dry capture might look like for one of the poses we've just seen.

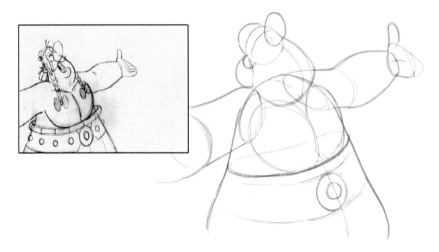

FIGURE 2.3 *Dry capturing is about structure: seeing the whole as an arrangement of its parts.*

With this approach, you're no longer capturing the properties of the subject as whole. Instead, you're analyzing its *structure*. I call these *dry captures*, because of their logical and factual nature.

What would a dry capture look like in a different medium?

Writers, for example, dry-capture their stories with a bulleted list called an *outline*. Here, an entire fairy tale is captured through four simple lines:

- Mom sends Little Red Riding Hood to forest.
- LRRH gets lost, meets wolf, learns about grandma.
- Red Riding Hood gets to grandma's house, doesn't recognize wolf, gets eaten.
- Hunter kills wolf, saves LRRH and grandma.

CAPTURE | CONCEPT | VISION | PRODUCTION | PLAN |

How would you simplify the Eiffel Tower using dry capturing? Again, there isn't a single "correct" answer. Although this is a more objective way of capturing, it still relies on choice and taste. For example, I can dry-capture it as a three-part structure (Figure 2.4A), but I can also capture it as four converging parts joined together with arcs (Figure 2.4B). Both of these interpretations are correct, and both are easily recognizable as the Eiffel Tower.

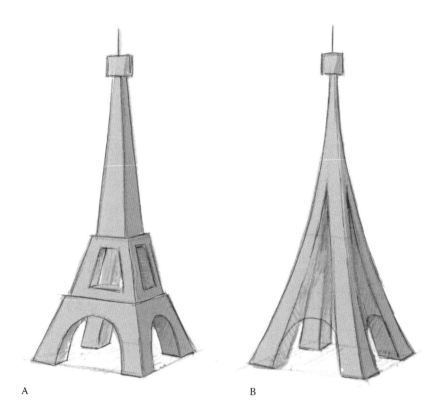

A   B

FIGURE 2.4 *Dry-capturing is a matter of choice, too. Is the Eiffel tower made of three shapes built one or top of the other (A) or four converging arcs (B)?*

The wet and dry approaches are rooted deep in the very structure of our brain. You might have heard of it referred to as *right-brain thinking* and *left-brain thinking*. I'll expand on this subject in Chapter 3.

CAPTURE

CONCEPT | VISION | PRODUCTION | PLAN |

A Splash of Details

So far, we've been talking about capturing in terms of broad strokes. With both wet and dry captures, we have stripped down our subjects and ignored their finer details and texture. But the details are often an important part of what makes a subject fascinating in the first place. How can we add them in without losing the simplicity and speed of the capture?

Here's one way. In Figure 2.5, sketch A is a very basic dry capture of a structure. In sketch B, I've added in a few details.

A   B

FIGURE 2.5 *Just a few details added to a "boring" dry-capture can make a big difference.*

Notice that even though there is only a small difference between the sketches, sketch B feels a lot richer and full of character. That's because I cheated: I added just the right amount of information for your brain to engage and start filling in the gaps, imagining a much fuller experience than is actually there. The human brain is very good at that kind of thing, and it also happens to enjoy the exercise. That's why captures, like minimalistic art, have a special kind of charm to them—a quality that is often lost in the fully rendered and polished work.

What happens if I add more details to my capture? Let's give it a try.

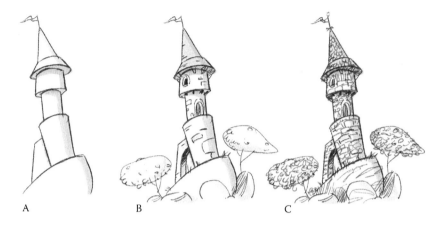

A   B   C

FIGURE 2.6   *Drawing (C) is worse than (B), even though it has more details.*

As you can see in Figure 2.6, the extra details did not improve the capture. Instead of being suggestive, it bombards your brain with excessive information, and the result feels tedious and busy. Details are a strong spice: just a small amount can make an unexciting dish taste great, but add too much, and it becomes uneatable.

On top of that, this kind of detailed sketch simply takes too long to do and thus loses the focused energy of a quick capture.

To conclude: for a quick capture that combines focus, simplicity, and appeal, start with big-picture thinking (using either wet or dry capturing) and then carefully add just enough details to get the audience's brain engaged.

Exaggeration

In capturing your point of view clearly and quickly, exaggeration makes a valuable tool. The idea is simple: you allow yourself to distort the subject, in order to boldly put forward its most important features. It's very much like making a caricature of what you're describing.

CAPTURE | CONCEPT | VISION | PRODUCTION | PLAN |

Again, the Eiffel Tower sketches make a good example. In Figure 2.7, the point is made that the tower's design feels *jaunty*.

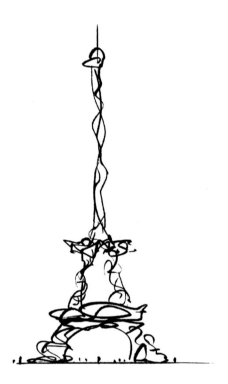

FIGURE 2.7   *"Jaunty" sketch of Eiffel Tower.*

Even though the real tower is obviously not as jaunty as *that*, it's still easily recognizable, and the personal point of view is put forward very clearly.

In the storyboard panel in Figure 2.8, from the TV series *Shaun the Sheep*, I drew an exaggerated pose to make the clear visual statement that Shaun is pushing down hard. In the final animated shot, it had been toned down quite a bit*. That's because in the final animation, the movement of the character already clarifies what he's doing, and along with music, color, lighting, and sound

---

* For those of you interested in comparing the boards with the final animation, the episode's name is "Bagpipe Buddy."

FIGURE 2.8   *The exaggerated storyboard helped clarify the idea. Later, they toned it down and allowed the movement and sound carried it through.*

effects, the action is made clear to the audience without having to be exaggerated. Still, in the process of making the film, it is helpful that the storyboard expresses the action so clearly.

To hammer the point home, Figure 2.9 shows the capture I made for that same panel, that is, the super-fast sketch I did in preparation for the final drawing. This was a very quick doodle, done in no more than a few seconds. How do you communicate an idea *that* quickly? By spitting out your most instinctive and raw impression and *exaggerating* that point as much as possible.

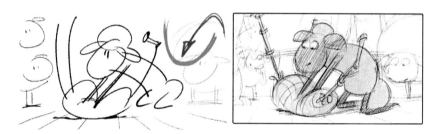

FIGURE 2.9   *Exaggeration and wet-capturing were used for planning the storyboards before drawing the final panels. The red/blue lines were not part of the original sketch—I've added them here to show the exaggerated thought even more clearly. It's a capture-of-a-capture-of-a-capture!*

Condensing and Expanding

Simplification and minimalism come at many different levels. We just saw an example of that with the storyboard sketches: both drawings are captures, both are simplifications, but one of them is a much more *condensed* capture. That provides you with another handy tool: condensing and expanding your captures.

CAPTURE | CONCEPT | VISION | PRODUCTION | PLAN |

Expanding Your Capture

You can start with a super-quick capture and then gradually expand it so it's more accessible to others. I often use this technique when I need to focus my attention on big picture issues. Once I'm happy with the way the big picture turned out, I can turn my attention to expanding my capture with less essential details.

The storyboard shown earlier is an example of that: I started out with a series of *very* raw sketches, focusing my entire attention on big-picture story issues. Once that was in place, I gradually expanded my captures, adding details and finesse.

This approach work particularly well with *placeholders*, which we'll discuss in Section VI.

Condensing

In other situations, you'll want to go the opposite way and *condense* your capture. That is, start with a more detailed version, then make it leaner. This is a great technique for figuring out the very core of your subject—something that's not always easy to do right off the bat.

Here's an example. Screenwriters often use a specific kind of capture called a *logline*—a brief description of the entire film, usually only one or two sentences long. Put yourself in the screenwriter's shoes for a moment. You've spent weeks, perhaps months, developing your script—solving problems, coming up with funny moments, creating fun characters, and putting together all the little twists and turns of the plot and subplots. You have an intimate knowledge of the story, and what's more, your care about it too much. It's can be really tough for you to judge what is and isn't essential at this point.

In such a case, it makes sense to start with a more expanded capture and then "capture the capture" a few times, until you get to the heart-of-the-core-of-the-essence of your subject (Figure 2.10).

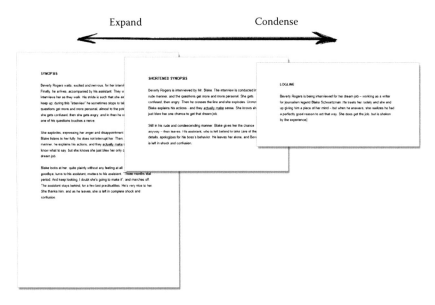

FIGURE 2.10　*Simplifying one step at a time, from a half-page synopsis to a single paragraph logline. You can also do it the other way: start with a logline and gradually expand it to a more elaborated synopsis.*

Practice Makes Perfect

You now have a set of tools for effective capturing. I hope you're excited about giving them a try!

You can start implementing these techniques in your daily creative work right away, but I suggest that you take some time to do simple, standalone capture exercises. It will give you the freedom to experiment freely, without the stress and confusion of a live project.

So, how do you practice capturing?

Simple: pick a few interesting subjects and describe them as quickly and as clearly as you can—just like the exercise we started Chapter 1 with. The medium is not important since what we're practicing here is not so much craft as a certain *mental approach*. Focus on the techniques we've just gone through: expand and contract your captures, use exaggeration to see how far you can push things, and try adding or taking away details to see how much is too much.

The subjects you capture could be literally anything: people around you in a coffee shop, a frame from a film you love, something you've read, a memory, or even just a feeling. Whatever grabs your interest is a good subject. All you have to do is figure out *why* it grabbed your interest, and there's your capture!

As you practice, make sure you experiment with both dry and wet captures. Try to find out which one comes more naturally to you. This is important, since the concept of wet vs. dry—intuition vs. analysis—is one of the keys to a healthy creative workflow.

In the next chapter, we'll take a deeper look at these two powerful forces of creativity.

CAPTURE

CONCEPT | VISION | PRODUCTION | PLAN |

Chapter 3

The Dual-Thinking Engine

I've always been fascinated with three-dimensional sight. You know how that works: each eye sees the world from a slightly different angle, and your brain uses the difference between the two angles to create an illusion of depth. What you end up experiencing is not two separate pictures, but one enhanced picture.

Similarly, even though we may *feel* we perceive the world through a single mental point of view, we actually don't. Our perception is made up of the combined perceptions of our two hemispheres: the right hemisphere and the left hemisphere. This is a physical thing: two actual lumps of gray matter that live side by side in the skull, talking to each other through a kind of "communication bridge."

From here on, I'll call the two hemispheres *the right brain* and *the left brain*, since for the purpose of our discussion, they really do function like two separate organs.

Each of our "brains" has a completely different way of interpreting the world. The left brain uses *logic*. The right brain uses *intuition*.

Since capturing is a way of communicating your personal *interpretation* of a subject, the fact that you have two parallel interpretation devices—and that your audience has the same—is relevant to our discussion of capture. Your "two brains" are literally your most important creativity tools, and it makes a lot of sense to know exactly what they can do, what they can't do, and when to use each one.

The Dry Capture

Let's start with the left brain.

Your left brain is excellent at detecting *structure*. This means it's good at taking a subject apart, understanding each part separately, noting how the parts relate to each other, and then putting the whole thing back together again. I call these left-brain captures *dry captures*, because they keep you emotionally detached from the subject (Figure 3.1). You create them by asking yourself, "how do I *understand* this? What *parts* is it made of?"

FIGURE 3.1   *In this, my left brain perceived the main body of the pear as a cone mounted on a ball. It also identified three color tones: main color, shade, and highlight.*

You'll see this kind of thinking in textbooks teaching any kind of art form. Any decent book about writing, for example, will teach you how to write an outline—a bulleted list of your main story beats. That outline is a form of dry capturing, because you're basically asking yourself: "what is my story made of? How do I break it down to simpler parts?"

CAPTURE

CONCEPT | VISION | PRODUCTION | PLAN |

The exact same thinking process is applied when sketching a website's wireframe (Figure 3.2): it's a quick and rough dry capture that answers the question "what parts is this web page made of?"

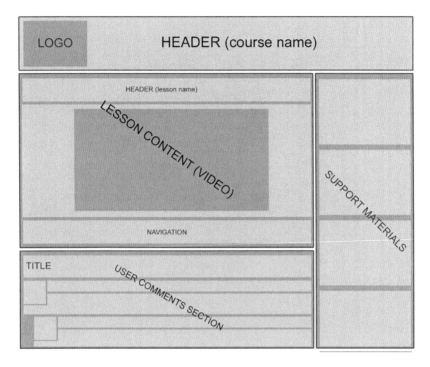

FIGURE 3.2 Dry capturing in web design. "What parts is this web page made of?"

Why Go Dry?

What's great about capturing with your left brain? The following highlights some of the main advantages.

Control

Dry captures are a cool, calm, and collected way of working. No mess, no frustration, no fuss: you're in control of the situation. Like a hardened general on the battlefield, you keep yourself emotionally detached and composedly make your decisions.

A friend of mine—a very experienced animator—is a complete left-brain guy. I used to watch in envy as he sat there, leaned back, calmly charting his left-brain captures. He was doing hundreds of drawings without throwing out a single sheet of paper, while I—being more of a right-brain kind of animator—was desperately scribbling, searching, trying, waiting for something to finally "click," as crumpled papers pile up around me (Figure 3.3).

FIGURE 3.3 *The cool, calm, and collected left brain work vs. the messy emotional right brain work.*

Dry captures are technically accurate, measurable, almost scientific in nature. They are more predictable than wet captures: you can estimate quite accurately how much time they'll take to make. Because they're about breaking down the subject to parts, they help you plan your work and make your deadlines (Figure 3.4). Put all that together, and it amounts to a dependable creative workflow.

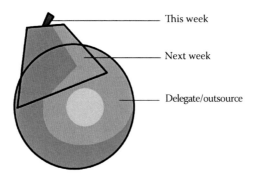

This week

Next week

Delegate/outsource

FIGURE 3.4 *Dry captures make it easier to plan your work and make your deadlines.*

CAPTURE | CONCEPT | VISION | PRODUCTION | PLAN |

Structure

Structure is an important tool for clear communication in any medium. Take this book for example: imagine the exact same book, but without sentences, chapters, or paragraphs, just one long string of words and images. It would have been challenging to get anything out of such a book—even though the information is all there.

Because dry captures are about recognizing the different parts of a subject, they tend to add *structure* to your work and thereby improve clarity.

Logic

Dry-capturing is based on logic, which makes it easier to explain to others what you do and why you do it. Thus, being good at dry-capturing paves your way to teaching and supervising positions.

Editability

Perhaps the most powerful advantage of dry captures is that they're easy to edit. Look at the pear capture in Figure 3.5, for example. Because of the structural nature of the dry sketch, I can easily make changes: move elements around, delete them, modify them, change relationships between parts, and so on. Not happy with a change I've made? No problem: I can easily change it back. Wet captures don't offer anything close to that kind of flexibility.

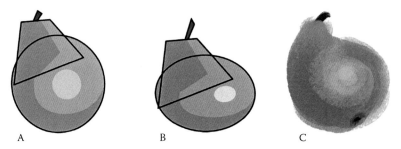

A   B   C

FIGURE 3.5 *Version A is my original dry capture. In version B, I made the highlight whiter, I squashed the lower part and added some red to the base color of the pear. This was all done in just a few seconds. The wet capture (C) does not allow that kind of modular editing.*

CAPTURE | CONCEPT | VISION | PRODUCTION | PLAN |

To sum up: dry captures are great for when you need control and overview. They are practical, professional, reliable, and they give you a great deal of flexibility.

Now, let's turn to wet-capturing and see what the right side of your brain has to offer.

The Wet Capture

Your right brain is the exact opposite of your left brain. It doesn't take things apart, but rather perceives them as a whole. It sees the world through emotions and in light of your past experiences.

To activate your wet-capturing engine, ask yourself: "How do I *feel* about this?" or "What does this *remind me of*?"

FIGURE 3.6   *Wet capture version of the pear.*

These are the questions I asked myself before I made the wet capture of the pear in Figure 3.6. Oddly, the pear made me think of a spiral— a bit like the number 6. The colors made me think of cool springtime sun shining on a green meadow. So, that's what I tried to capture.

You can see how this is an entirely different approach than the "cone mounted on ball" capture produced by the left brain. It's messy and sticky and juicy; a *wet* capture indeed. It's also a perception of the pear as a whole—something that is greater and more meaningful than the sum if its parts.

Why Go Wet?

We've seen the strong advantages of dry capturing. What are some of the advantages of wet captures?

Visceral

Wet captures are exciting, emotional, involved, and passionate. Even when they're not perfect, people connect with them. They don't just understand them—they enjoy them. They laugh, or they say "Aww, that's so cute!" or they connect with the story the capture tells. In many ways, they're what art is all about.

Dynamic

The holistic nature of wet captures creates a coherent flow, unbroken by sections, chapters, and dividers. Things move naturally from one area to the next, and there's dynamic energy and charm to that (Figure 3.7).

A   B

FIGURE 3.7   *The left-brain capture (A) has a clear structure, but the right brain capture (B) has flow, energy, and life.*

CAPTURE   CONCEPT | VISION | PRODUCTION | PLAN |

Surprising

Wet captures are where surprises and happy accidents happen. You never know what's going to come out of a wet capture; you're not really driving this. It can turn out a miserable mess, but it can also be the most beautiful thing you've ever made; and you'll be looking at it thinking, "where did *that* come from?!"

Creative

Wet captures are creative, in the sense that they add something to the mix that wasn't there before: new associations, analogies, unexpected connections. Most importantly, they add something of *you* to the work—you as an individual person, with your own personal story. Wet captures are not about what you know—they're about who you *are* and what you've been through in life. That's a powerful ingredient to add to your work.

To sum up: wet captures are good for adding some zest to your work. You use them to connect with your audience, to make them laugh, to surprise them. Dry captures may be easy to follow, but it's wet captures that'll make your audience fall in love with your work.

Is the Left Brain Evil?

The left brain has a bad reputation with creatives because of its tendency to judge and criticize—especially when things get a bit "experimental." Admittedly, the left brain does represent a strict, no-fooling-around kind of approach: "what's right is right, what's wrong is wrong." That's not always helpful, because at its highest level, creativity requires a good deal of fooling around. Thus, more than a few books have been written that urge readers to completely shut out their left brain and rely solely on their lenient right brain.

To me, this is a strange advice. What about all the wonderful advantages of left-brain thinking? Structure, clarity, control, editing—are we ready to toss those aspects of creativity to the waste bin? It also defies common sense: we have two amazingly powerful perception tools at our disposal. Why on earth would we want to ignore one of them entirely?

Clearly, we have those two interpretation systems for a reason. They complete each other perfectly, like yin and yang: the advantages of one are the exact drawbacks of the other, and vice versa. Just like having two eyes gives our sight depth, these two systems—when used in unison—give us a depth of perception that is not achievable using just one of them.

Is it true that these two thinking engines can become conflicted, work against each other, and end up harming your work? Sure, it happens all the time. But is this really a good reason to simply discard half your brainpower? Seems to me that a better advice would be to learn how to *synergize* your two brains. In other words: to become an expert at getting them to work well together.

Synergy Techniques

The following are three different approaches for getting your right and left brain to collaborate rather than compete. I call them *layering*, *clustering*, and *blending*.

Layering

With this method, you layer your captures in such a way that you're switching between right-brain and left-brain thinking with each layer. This works great when combined with the *working in passes* technique, which we'll discuss in detail in Section V.

FIGURE 3.8 *(A) Left brain, (B) right brain, (C) left brain.*

Figure 3.8 shows you how layering works in principle: (A) is the first layer, which is a dry capture in this case (clear and logical). Then you build on it with a layer of *wet* capture—an intuitive flow (B). Then you can add another *dry layer* (C) for clarity and style. The final result has a good mix of dry and wet: it combines flow, structure, randomness, and clarity.

Figure 3.9 shows an example of the same idea, used to capture our pear image:

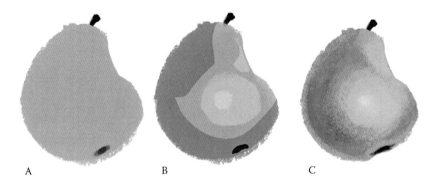

FIGURE 3.9 *(A) Wet—no structure, only an intuitive shape; (B) dry capture layered on top—capturing light and shade in a structural, logical way; (C) layers in a wet capture again.*

Clustering

With clustering, you're taking the modular property of dry-capturing and using it to inject some wet-capturing. The idea is to *build a dry capture out of wet captures.*

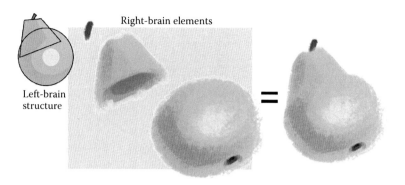

FIGURE 3.10   *Clustering: a dry series of wet captures.*

In this example (Figure 3.10), the pear has three parts. As you know by now, that's left-brain thinking. Here, however, each part is represented with a vibrant and messy right-brain capture. The result is a work that *feels* wet but has a lot of the control of dry thinking: it's logical and structured, and I can still work on each part separately.

Here's another example. Figure 3.11 is a series of thumbnails that capture an animated shot. Each pose, in and of itself, is a messy wet capture (you can see how the drawings are focused on emotion rather than structure). However, as a capture for an animated shot, the *series* of drawings shows a left-brain approach. Each wet sketch is an element in the dry structure and can be deleted, replaced, rearranged, or modified.

FIGURE 3.11   *Clustering in animation: a controlled set of messy poses.*

Let's look at how clustering works in writing. This bulleted outline is, of course, a dry capture. However, in and of itself, every beat is a wet capture: not a dry and factual description, but an emotional and messy representation of that part in the story.

- *Large room, very corporate. Beverly waiting for interview, nervous, she really wants that job.*
- *Interview starts. Boss is a famous figure, she admires him. Gives her a hard time—she gets confused, then frustrated, then angry.*
- *He crosses a line—she EXPLODES! Lets him have it. We're totally on her side...*
- *He gives a steady answer: "this is my way of learning if you can handle talking to big shots."*
- *Beverly (and us) STUNNED that he actually has a good reason. She blew it...*
- *He gives her a chance (but predicts she won't make it).*

Blending

The simplest approach to describe is also the toughest to implement: blending simply means that you work with both brains at the same time, keeping an elegant balance of wet and dry thinking. Don't be discouraged if it doesn't work for your right away: this synergy approach requires quite a bit of experience and practice.

In the series of poses in Figure 3.12, each drawing uses both left-brain clarity and right-brain flow. The holistic thinking is marked red: "stretched," "forward arch," "backward arch," and so on. At the same time, each drawing also contains the analytical, structural left-brain thinking (marked blue).

FIGURE 3.12 *Pirate jump blending. Each drawing in the series is a blend of left brain logic and structure, with right brain fluidity and energy.*

Balance Your Brains

I ended the last chapter advising you to experiment with wet and dry captures and to figure out which one you naturally lean toward. As we've learned in this chapter, true creative strength lies not in choosing one thinking mode over the other but in creating balance and synergy between them. A creative with 100% skill on one side of the brain and 0% skill on the other side will be considerably worse off than a creative with an equal 50% skill on both sides.

So, once you realize which side of your brain you're more comfortable capturing with, my advice is to focus on building up the *other* side. If dry capturing comes easy to you, practice capturing with your *intuition* for a while. If wet capturing is your usual dish, focus your exercises on *analytical* captures. Once you feel reasonably balanced, experiment with the synergy techniques and get used to capturing with both your thinking engines.

The better you get at doing this, the better your captures will get—and the smoother your overall creative workflow will become.

Before we conclude this section and go into the actual creative workflow, let's go over a few safety rules to help you avoid the common pitfalls of capturing.

CAPTURE | CONCEPT | VISION | PRODUCTION | PLAN |

Chapter 4

The Capture Safety Rules

Focus on Communication— Not Craft

A live-action director I worked with briefly used to explain his ideas with little sketches. He was not a good draftsman and kept apologizing for it. The truth was, his captures—unattractive as they were—always made complete sense to me. They allowed me to understand exactly what he had envisioned, quickly and with almost no back-and-forth required.

Sometimes, captures are attractive. Sometimes they're not. The truth is, it doesn't matter. Capturing is about clarity, communication, focus, and speed—not about dazzling someone with your craft.

In fact, an attractive capture is not always an advantage. An impressive capture can "sell" a bad idea—something I've seen happen more than once. On the flip side, if you can sell an idea with a very basic capture, you can be confident that the idea itself is working. For that reason, I often do "ugly" captures *on purpose*— just to make sure people are not distracted by the craft.

Ironically, when you stop trying to create attractive captures and start focusing on expressing your ideas clearly, your captures often get more attractive. There is beauty in clarity and focus.

The safety rule: when capturing, don't worry about craftsmanship. Focus on expressing your ideas clearly.

Don't Invest Too Much Effort

As creatives, it is in our nature to want to delve into things. We're the perfect geeks of whatever it is we're interested in. It's part of what makes us good at what we do.

For many of us, the temptation to delve into a capture and spend more time on it than we absolutely need to can be hard to resist: "I'll just add *this* cool detail," "let me just fix *that* annoying mistake."

This goes against what capturing is all about, not just because it takes away speed and focus but also because of something called the "sunk cost fallacy." It's been proven that the more resources we put into something, the less open we are to the possibility of it being wrong. It creates a premature commitment, and a big part of why we capture an idea in the first place is to try it *before* we commit to it.

It should therefore be your active goal to invest as little time and effort as possible in your captures. There is real power in the idea of capturing your thoughts as quickly and as simply as you can.

The safety rule: when in doubt, do less! Make it your goal to invest as little effort as possible in your captures.

Don't Limit Yourself to Your Comfort Medium

Writers feel comfortable with words; painters feel comfortable with paint; 3D artists feel comfortable with a 3D design software. That's just natural. However, you should be aware that your natural go-to medium may not always be the best choice for the particular subject your capturing. Some ideas lend themselves to verbal description. Other ideas are better represented visually. Capturing in 2D (e.g., sketching) may be too limiting for some ideas, making a 3D medium (e.g., clay, a 3D software, or even Lego) the better choice. Sometimes *timing* is a big part of the idea, in which case a video or an audio capture may be required.

Experience will teach you which medium would work better in each case (and for you personally), but the main idea is to stay open to alternative capturing possibilities. If you're a writer, don't be afraid to capture with sketches. If you're a character designer, maybe it makes sense to use clay as one of your capturing tools. You may not be proficient in that other medium; don't worry about that. Remember that a capture doesn't need to be attractive or well crafted to be effective. It just needs to get the idea across.

Being open to different options also means you can get creative with the way you capture your ideas. For instance, I've seen game designers build game levels out of Lego—an ingenious way to communicate their ideas quickly and inexpensively in a way that allows quick editing. Some web designers use pieces of cardboard to quickly try out different designs. On a few occasions, I have used a phone camera and random objects to speed up my storyboarding process, especially when trying to capture a difficult camera move. Those are all unconventional, but highly effective, capturing mediums.

Finally, for maximum speed and clarity, try combining several mediums in your captures. Draw over photos, combine text with images, use 2D sketches as part of your 3D capture—whatever gives you the most speed and clarity is the right way to go.

The safety rule: don't limit yourself to familiar mediums and techniques. The only things that matter are clarity and speed.

Conclusion

This concludes our in-depth capture section. If this is your first read, I hope it made sense to you; it should make even more sense as you read on. If this is *not* your first read, I hope you see how these concepts and tips provide a solid foundation for the methods explained hereafter.

Remember to practice your capturing regularly. It is the easiest skill to get better at: captures don't take long to do (by definition), don't require fancy equipment, and can be done virtually anywhere. You can practice during your coffee break, your daily commute, while watching TV, and even during long meetings. It's going to be worth your while: captures are the basic building blocks of creativity—which is why you're going see them pop up everywhere in the next few sections. That means that every tiny improvement in your ability to capture gets multiplied over and over throughout your workflow, which will have a significant effect on the quality of your work.

And now, finally, it's time to go into the creative workflow itself. We'll start—as is appropriate—at the very beginning: the blank page.

AT A GLANCE:

THE CAPTURE

A concise representation
of a more detailed subject

**THE CREATIVE ATOM:
EVERY WORK IS ESSENTIALLY
A STRUCTURE OF CAPTURES**

TECHNIQUES

GET PERSONAL
BASIC FORM + JUST A FEW DETAILS
EXAGGERATION
COMPRESS/EXPAND

DRY CAPTURES
(LEFT HEMISPHERE)

"How do I understand this?"
"What is it made of?"

- CONTROLLED
- EDITABLE
- STRUCTURED

WET CAPTURES
(RIGHT HEMISPHERE)

"How do I feel about this?"
"What does it remind me of?"

- EXCITING
- CREATIVE
- FLOWING

SYNERGY TECHNIQUES
WET+DRY TOGETHER

LAYERING: SWITCH BETWEEN WET AND DRY
CLUSTERING: CREATE A DRY SET OF WET CAPTURES
BLENDING: USE BOTH THINKING MODE SIMULTANEOUSLY

THE CONCEPT

From a Blank Page to
An Exciting Core Idea

"To have a great idea, have a lot of them."

Thomas A. Edison

Chapter 5

The Blank Page

In the beginning, there is always the blank page.

Nothing is more disconcerting for the creative mind than having all the options completely open. Where do you begin? How do you make something out of nothing? It's all fun and games when inspiration hits right out of the blue, but how do you get it to strike on schedule? How do you come up with a great idea on demand?

To answer that question, we need to first get a clear view on how the magic of inspiration works.

The Mechanics of Inspiration

Imagine your brain as a huge storage room, to which random stuff is added all the time. Everything you see, hear, think about, imagine, dream, or learn goes into that mental storage room. It's a dynamic place, where these random pieces of data constantly move around, bump into each other, react to each other in different ways, and occasionally connect.

Let's say you happen to watch a TV show about fish. It's a bit boring and your mind starts wandering. The program brings up an old memory of a two-day fishing trip you went on, in which you saw a bear by the lake. Some hours later, you find yourself absently humming *The Bear Necessities*, and you're not sure why.

The idea of "bear" sticks around for a while, hovering at the edges of your subconscious mind. As you go through life, your brain tries to connect that "bear" thought to other pieces of information that float around your mental storage room. Then, a random conversation with a friend connects with "bear"; this triggers more thoughts, more associations, and in a split second—*seemingly* out of nowhere—an idea explodes into your head. The idea doesn't even have anything to do with a bear, but "bear" was certainly part of how it came about.

This is just a random thing that's going to happen to you every now and again, especially if your mind—like mine—tends to wander a lot. In that sense, inspiration isn't any more magical than finding some money on the pavement. It feels great when it happens, but ultimately, it's just blind luck.

Many creatives are not aware of that mental process. To many of us, the idea really did just appear out of nowhere, and we get used to thinking of great ideas as something "magical." It's quite understandable, therefore, that when asked to come up with a specific kind of idea, on schedule, and on budget, we freak out. How on earth do you get an idea to strike? We sit there, staring at the blank page, and desperately wait for the "magic" of inspiration to happen. In the best-case scenario, an idea does pop up, and then we gratefully take whatever we were given and consider ourselves lucky. In the worst-case scenario, the magic fails to happen, and then we end up using some cliché solution we don't even like.

That's not really a method, of course. The chances of just the right kind of "mental accident" happening exactly where and when you need it to, and being genuinely good on top of that, are not very high. A professional creative relying on inspiration for ideas is like someone trying to make a living by walking around looking for money on the pavement.

Generating Magic

So, how do you stop relying on inspiration for ideas, and what do you replace it with?

The secret is to use *captures* to move the process out of your head and onto your desktop, expanding your capacity, and giving you more control. Then, use these captures to deliberately create the conditions that would make a stroke of "random" inspiration inevitable.

The entire workflow comes down to three main steps:

Step 1. Capture a bunch of random thoughts and bits of ideas.

Step 2. Let these thoughts bump into each other and form exciting options.

Step 3. Consolidate it all to one exciting core idea.

This may sound quite simple, and in fact it is—when you know how to do it. In the next few chapters, we're going to discuss each step in turn, and I'll give you all the tools you need to make this workflow every bit as smooth and enjoyable as it can be.

Ideas vs. Concepts

Before we continue I'd like to clear up a possible source of confusion. In the list above step 1 may seem absurd: coming up with ideas is exactly the problem. How can it also be part of the solution?

To resolve that contradiction, let's define the difference between an *idea* and a *concept* (Figure 5.1).

For our purposes, *an idea* is any scrap of thought you come up with as you think creatively about your subject. It doesn't have to be good, or complete, or smart, or even coherent. If you can think it, it's an idea.

For example, say you're working on a story that involves a shepherd. Your first thought could be something like, "Maybe he has a flute." That's an idea. Your second thought could be, "maybe he's awful at playing it, and his sheep hate it when he plays." That's another idea. Are they *good* ideas? Yes, they are—in the sense that they provide *options* for you to work with. Whether you're going to end up using them or not is a different matter.

A *concept* is something much more substantial. It is a viable solution to your creative challenge—a core idea that you can build your entire piece around. In other words, a concept is exactly the sort of thing people expect inspiration to bestow on them, as they stare at that blank page.

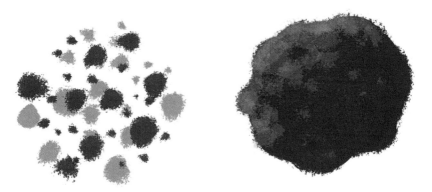

FIGURE 5.1   *A bunch of ideas vs. a full concept.*

So, when someone says "I don't have any ideas," what they really mean is "I can't come up with a good enough concept." To which I say: well, what if you don't have to come up with a concept at all? Can you come up with some bits of thoughts? Bad ideas? Crazy ideas? Stupid ideas? Incoherent, abstract, far-fetched ideas? If you're a living, functioning human being, the answer to that is always "yes." In fact, I guarantee you that the amount of raw ideas you can come up with on any given subject is virtually unlimited.

FIGURE 5.2 A bunch of ideas *for a story involving a disagreement over an egg. Some of these are so random, they hardly even make sense. The color drawing is the* concept *that came out of those ideas: paternity dispute between a rooster and a hen.*

A 10-Minute Exercise

Let's try it now with a quick exercise—just to give you a taste of what it feels like to come up with random ideas.

Exotica Animal Fashion is a fictional company that designs clothing and accessories for exotic animals. That's right—if you have a koala for a pet, Exotica will help you make it hip.

Your job is to come up with a concept for something that would help Exotica—something you know how to do. You can pretend you're designing their website or their logo, creating an app, writing a short story about it, composing a catchy jingle, designing one of their products—whatever works for you.

Take 10 minutes or so, and try to quickly capture any thought that comes to your mind regarding this imaginary project.

The exercise is deliberately silly: I want you to take it lightly and have some fun with this. Make a real effort to let your ideas flow freely; don't judge or second-guess them. Remember that you're not looking for *good* ideas at this point: it's quantity, not quality, that's going to win the day. At the end of the 10 minutes, you should have a pile of papers full of captured bits of thoughts.

An Endless Stream of Ideas

After tossing these bits of random thoughts around for a while, you'll inevitably get to a point where the stream of ideas dries out. You can't think of anything else to add—not even a bad idea comes to mind. You've emptied your mental storage room.

Except you haven't. Not yet.

Often, it's just a sign that you've exhausted your pool of *easy* ideas— the ones that come readily to mind. Those are the obvious ideas, the clichés, the kind of ideas you've been conditioned to come up with by culture and habit and existing formulas. That's good! It means you're at the brink of a new kind of ideas—refreshing, off-the-beaten-path ideas, that you yourself may be surprised by. The key to success is to persevere, and to venture beyond the comfort zone of "acceptable ideas."

But even that has a limit, doesn't it? No matter how determined and adventurous you are, sooner or later, you're bound to get to a point at which, try as you may, there are no more ideas you can think of. You're done.

Except you're not. Not yet.

Allow me to repeat: no matter what the subject is, there is a practically infinite number of ideas and thoughts you can come up with. If you can't find these ideas, that's not because they're not there. It's because you're not looking at the right place.

In the next chapter, I'll teach you how to expand your search, open hidden doors in your mental storage room, and gain access to more ideas than you ever thought you had in you.

CAPTURE CONCEPT VISION | PRODUCTION | PLAN

Chapter **6**

Breaking Your Thinking Patterns

Let's start with a recap of what we're trying to accomplish here.

We're at the first step of our three-step process, which is going to create the conditions for inspiration to strike when and where you need it. In this step, your goal is to come up with as many ideas as possible—and by "idea," I mean "anything that comes to mind." You've done that for a while and now you're stuck: you can't think of anything else to add.

Let me tell you a silly little story that may help you see the problem in a new way.

I used to play a computer game called *Unreal Tournament.* In case you have no idea what I'm talking about: imagine a complex building, full of winding corridors running between floors and sections and rooms and doors and elevators and so on. As the player, you run around collecting weapons, ammo, and other items that you can then use against other players.

There was a level in the game in which a special weapon was hidden somewhere—the most powerful weapon in the game.

CAPTURE | CONCEPT | VISION | PRODUCTION | PLAN

I knew for certain it was there because other players were using it. I tried every corridor and every door I saw—but I couldn't find that weapon. After spending way too much time on this, I suddenly took a turn and found myself in a corridor I'd never been to before. The odd thing is that it wasn't hidden or anything: I missed it simply because I kept turning right instead of left at a certain junction. I did this over and over again, even though I was actively trying to avoid repetition. I was stuck in a hidden *pattern*.

When I finally turned left and broke the pattern, I found myself in an entirely new area. I was excited. Surely the secret weapon is here!

It wasn't.

You know what happens next, don't you? I found another pattern I was stuck in; then another one, then another. Every time I thought I had taken every possible path, it turned out I still had more blind spots—created by my own subconscious patterns. I did eventually find the special weapon, but it took a while.

The Hidden Corridors of Your Mind

I hope you see where I'm going with this. Metaphorically speaking, your mental storage room is a similar place: strange and complex, full of crazy corridors and doors and unexpected passageways—only much, *much* more complex than any game has ever been. When you're out of ideas, it's not because there are no more ideas in your head. It's because you're stuck in a repetitive thinking pattern. Once you find a way to break that pattern, you'll discover a whole new area—and a new stream of ideas will start flowing.

Breaking patterns isn't necessarily easy, of course. As shown in my little game story, the problem is that you can't really see the pattern while you're in it. In the following pages, we'll go through a set of techniques designed to help you break your patterns and unlock new areas in your mental storage room.

Take a Break

The most basic pattern breaker you have at your disposal is just to go and do something completely different for a while. You can take a walk (my personal favorite), go have coffee with a colleague, maybe even play a game. The longer the break and the more successful you are in taking your mind off the problem, the better chance you have of breaking your pattern.

Make sure you don't take the break at your desk: Internet breaks won't work. You need to change your posture, your environment, your eyes' focus distance. Try to create as much contrast between your work state and your break state.

When the break is over, you can boost its effect by tackling the work a bit differently: take an alternative approach, change your tools (see next chapter), or shift your area or focus.

Change Your Tools

This pattern breaker is so simple that it is hard to believe it's as effective as it is. All you need to do is simply change the tools you're using for your capture. Drawing with a pencil will get you different ideas than drawing with a marker. If you're using a word processor, switch to pen and paper. If you're bilingual, try switching languages. If you've been composing with a piano, try switching to your guitar. By changing your tools, you'll be forcing your brain to break its patterns and see things differently.

I've also found it surprisingly helpful to change my working environment. Curiously, it has the same effect as changing your tool. Just moving to a different room or taking your work to the nearest coffee shop often makes a real difference.

On one of my recent projects, I was doing storyboards and was having difficulty connecting with my sequence. After a couple of hours of doodling ideas, I noticed I was going in circles: although I was actively trying to come up with new options, my brain kept repeating the same ideas—just like in the game story.

CAPTURE | CONCEPT | VISION | PRODUCTION | PLAN

Before developing these workflow methods, my reaction to a situation like this would be a complete meltdown: frustration, frantic sketching, more failure, more frustration, and so on. Not anymore: once I realized I was stuck in a pattern, I decided to change both my environment and my tools. I left my computer, took a pen and bunch of note cards, and went downstairs to the specious and brightly lit kitchen. Within one hour, I didn't just get new ideas—I actually had the entire storyboard solved and captured.

For an even stronger effect, you can try switching between mediums. If you've been writing story ideas, how about trying to sketch them? If you've been doodling character designs, how about using clay or a 3D program? Remember that you don't need to be proficient in a medium to create an effective capture. Switching mediums is almost guaranteed to unlock new corridors in your mental storage room, so it's well worth the extra effort.

Get Silly

One trick you can use to effectively break your thinking patterns is to be deliberately wrong: to get silly and allow yourself to come up with outrageous, weird, or stupid ideas.

This may not be as easy as it sounds: for many people, it can be surprisingly uncomfortable to be wrong—even when no one is watching.

Case in point: in one of my animation courses, the concluding exercise is the "springboard jump." Before starting to animate, the students are asked to come up with a funny or interesting twist to the jump. Oddly enough, usually more than half the class comes up with a variation on one of these concepts: the character slides and falls awkwardly, the character is afraid of the water, or the diving board is too high.

Why do so many bright and creative young minds converge to the same three basic ideas? To figure it out, I started asking the students to submit their process sketches. That's when the reason became instantly clear: the students who came up with cliché ideas were keeping to "reasonable" solutions. I could see in their sketches that they were playing it safe. But breaking patterns is all about *not* playing it safe. It's about taking risks and venturing out of your conceptual comfort zone.

I drew the examples in Figure 6.1 to show the students just how unlimited the options are if you don't mind being silly for a bit. These doodles are very rough, but if you look carefully, you should be able to identify some seriously weird ideas: jumping from a straw into a cup of Coke, an elephant on the springboard, a man under the board walking upside down, a model walking on the spring-board as if it was a catwalk, and a bunch of other stupid thoughts.

FIGURE 6.1   *A bunch of silly ideas for the springboard exercise.*

Admittedly, most of these are way too silly and/or complex to be real options for this exercise, but you never know where a thought might lead you. A silly idea will often turn out not to be silly at all, but fun and original. Even if it is indeed completely silly and unusable, it will often trigger ideas that *are* usable, or connect with other ideas to form a viable option you'd never have come up with without having that silly idea first.

Use External Pattern Breakers

So far, we've been focusing on *internal* pattern breakers. The next step is to look for *external* pattern breakers.

The easiest way to do this is to look around you and find a random object that has nothing to do with the idea you need, but that might start a train of associations that'll throw your mind off its established pattern. Figure 6.2 shows a simple example.

FIGURE 6.2   *This lamp broke my thinking pattern and gave me a fresh and interesting direction for a spaceship design.*

Of course, these days, you don't need to limit yourself to your room. You can go online and have instant access to an entire universe of information. This is both a blessing and a curse.

Let's stick to our cartoon spaceship example: what you *don't* want to do is to image-search "spaceship design." Instead of letting your brain connect with something random and unexpected, you'll be contaminating your thoughts with clichés and conventions. This is the exact opposite of what you want to achieve.

Instead, try searching for something that's either completely random or has a more associative connection to your actual subject. For the spaceship design example, I started by searching "alien" (associated with "spaceship"), which, for some reason, made me think of bugs. Maybe search for "alien bugs?" A bit of poking around that subject, and I got to some photos of bacteria and viruses. Look it up: they do tend to look like little spaceships floating in deep space, don't they?

Figure 6.3 shows a few design options inspired by that search.

FIGURE 6.3 *Spaceship designs inspired by microscopic organism.*

Harness More Brains

So far, we've been talking about methods to help you break your own thinking patterns all by yourself. You can go a long way doing that—but ultimately, the best and most powerful way to break your patterns is to involve other creative minds.

Entire books have been written about brainstorming and how to do it well, but the basic principle is very simple. Here's how it works.

The human brain is an association machine. Throw a thought at it and it produces several thoughts connected to it (Figure 6.4).

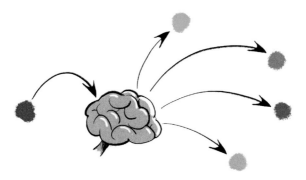

FIGURE 6.4 *Throw the brain a thought, and it'll produce several associations connected to it.*

We've just seen this in action with the previous spaceship example: "spaceship" triggered "aliens," which triggered "alien bugs."

When a group of people start throwing ideas at each other, this becomes a chain reaction: each idea triggers multiple ideas in different members of the group, those trigger even more ideas, and so on. The result is a "nuclear explosion" of thoughts and ideas (Figure 6.5).

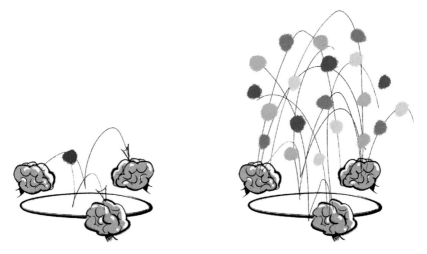

FIGURE 6.5 When a group of people throw ideas at each other, the result is a "nuclear explosion" of ideas.

A "brainstorming session" may sound intimidating, like something that involves a large group of people in a corporate meeting room. That's one way of doing it, but brainstorming can also be very simple. In its most basic form, you just grab a couple of friends and you shoot ideas at each other over a cup of coffee. To upgrade this from a casual creative chat to a formal, professional brainstorming session, all you'll need to do is implement four simple rules:

1. **Set a specific time frame for the meeting**. A predetermined time frame creates a sense of form and purpose and helps the participants take the rest of the rules more seriously. Make the session at least 30 minutes long: it takes time for the right kind of energy to build up. Don't make

it *too* long though: in my experience, after about 90 minutes, people start to lose their edge, and the session tends to dissolve to a bunch of people joking around. Fun, but not what we're after.

2. **Have someone capture the ideas**. As I've mentioned, a good brainstorming session is an exponential explosion of ideas. Trust me: you won't remember a thing. By capturing the ideas, you'll make sure you have every scrap of raw material available to you for the next step.

3. **No debates**. Debates over whether an idea is going to work or not are the kryptonite of brainstorming sessions. They cause people to seize up and withhold their most interesting ideas. Like the rest of the pattern-breaking techniques we've discussed, brainstorming is not about coming up with a viable concept. It's about generating interesting raw materials. Silly, wrong, and outrageous ideas should be allowed and even encouraged; don't let the group debate them. Capture all ideas, let them trigger other ideas, and move on.

4. **No problem solving**. At its best, brainstorming is a fast and furious process that moves through an incredible amount of different options in a short space of time. Don't let the session run aground by over-developing or solving a specific idea. Again, capture it and move on.

If you've done your brainstorming right, at the end of your 30- to 90-minute session, you'll have pages upon pages full of raw ideas—fresher, sillier, and more varied than anything you could have hoped to come up with by yourself; and each of these ideas has the potential to open up an exciting new area in your endless mental storage room.

Inspiration Sparks

This would be a good place to stop reading and continue the *Exotic Animal Fashion* exercise from the previous chapter.

Try breaking your patterns using the methods you've just learned. It doesn't matter which method you use first; just try whatever feels right to you. You can also use the same method more than once. Try doing this for another 20 minutes or so and see if you can make yourself laugh a little.

* * *

Breaking patterns is something you can basically do forever, and you'll always be able to come back with more. At some point, however, you're going to notice that your ideas start reacting to each other. Something you just thought of seems to relate to a silly idea someone tossed out at a brainstorming session; together, they create a completely new idea, which connects to a whole bunch of other thoughts you've captured. Things are starting to come together; solutions are starting to present themselves.

This is your cue that the raw materials stage is over. It's time to move on to step 2: forming concepts.

CAPTURE | CONCEPT | VISION | PRODUCTION | PLAN

Chapter 7

Forming Concepts

We started this section discussing the blank page anxiety and the problem of creating *something* out of *nothing*. Now that you've tossed around some raw ideas—this problem is gone: you're not staring at a blank page anymore. Instead, you're staring at a whole bunch of captured ideas that have already started reacting to each other and arranging themselves into viable solutions.

I call this stage the "idea soup": you've placed a bunch of ingredients in a pot, and now it's warming up and slowly turning into a delicious meal.

Daydream Mode

Since your raw ideas are already reacting to each other, you should let them continue to do that. Make sure you have your captured raw ideas in front of you and put yourself in "daydream mode". Let your thoughts run free. Ideas and concepts are going to assemble themselves, disassemble, morph, and then assemble again—all at breakneck speed. Daydreaming allows you to go through an astonishing amount of different options in a matter of seconds.

Don't try to steer or control this process too much, and don't try to make it happen any faster than it wants to. Inspiration is a wild animal; it will come to you, but only if you relax and give it time. If you chase it, it will run away.

I find that, after a while, gazing at the captured materials gets more confusing than helpful. At that point, I often leave the studio and go for a walk. The best concepts I came up with over the years materialized not in a studio, not in front of my computer or sketchbook, but in my head while walking. This is something I've heard repeatedly from other creatives as well. There's something about the combination of steady movement, constant yet mild external stimulus, and the circulation of blood that works as a catalyst for forming concepts.

Playing Lego

Daydream mode is super quick and agile, but it also has its drawbacks. Things happen so quickly it can get overwhelming. You could find yourself in a whirlwind of constructing and deconstructing concepts, without any of them getting enough time to solidify. Or, the exact opposite may happen: your brain could lock itself onto a certain concept, and refuse to try other options. This is all part of the lack of control that's inherent in doing things entirely in your head.

The alternative is an approach I'll call "playing Lego."

Have you played Lego as a kid? If you have, I assume you've done it more or less like I have: you'd spill the entire content of your Lego box on the floor around you and start putting random parts together, just to see what happens. Soon, some combination of parts would spark an idea—and you'd find yourself building a funky spaceship or a castle.

Find that kid inside of you again, because what we have here is the exact same process; except that now, instead of a bunch of Lego bricks, you have a bunch of captured raw ideas to play with. Start physically putting ideas together in different ways, see how they feel next to each other, then take them apart and try new combinations. Let your ideas morph and change in the process as needed. Again, the important thing is to keep it light and fun and not try to be too practical at this point. Don't force ideas to connect: the best results come from being playful and letting your concepts emerge naturally. Don't worry about making mistakes, too: if you get to a dead-end, just leave it and start over. If something feels like it's beginning to make sense, try building on it and see where it goes.

In the example in Figure 7.1 (a visualization of my real process developing a short script), the four ideas marked yellow made a lot of sense together—creating a loaded situation that felt potentially entertaining. From here on, the full concept almost created itself.

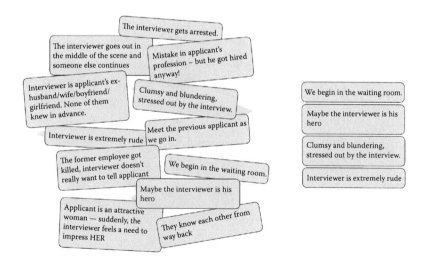

FIGURE 7.1   *Forming a concept from bits of ideas in screenwriting. Some people do work with actual physical cards like that; I prefer working with bulleted lists, copying/pasting around to try different combinations.*

This is obviously a much slower process than doing it in your head. On the plus side, you get to see what you're doing more clearly and it's easier to evaluate your emerging concepts. I also find that with this approach, weird and silly ideas get a better chance of pulling you in refreshing directions. When you work inside your head, your existing patterns will inevitably draw you toward more "comfortable" ideas.

As usual, I tend to combine both approaches. I start with day-dreaming to come up with a promising thread to pull on. Then, I "Lego around" with my captures to see where that thread leads to and to give weird ideas a chance. Then I go for a walk, and when I come back, I usually have a concept I'm really excited about.

I capture this first concept, set it aside - and then I do it all over again.

The First Concept Trap

Here's why it's important to never stop at your very first concept, exciting as it may be.

The time between starting to work on a project and the moment you have a clear concept for it can be rather unpleasant. It's a strange limbo situation, in which you're working on something without knowing what it actually is. Add a tight deadline to it, and you get a very strong need—both psychological and practical—to come up with something solid as fast as possible.

It's easy to see how, in that stressful situation, the first working concept you come up with can easily become a trap. Your mind wants to latch on to this first concept, and it *will* convince you that it is brilliant and that it's the best concept you can possibly come up with.

To avoid that trap, you need to capture that first concept as quickly as you can—and open your mind to try something else. You should assume that your first concept is wrong until proven otherwise. The only way to prove it *not* wrong is to have one or two other options to compare it with. Bear in mind that those other options should be distinctly different, not just minor variations on the first concept. Once you have two to three options to choose from, you're on safer ground.

Figure 7.2 shows a character design example from a TV commercial I worked on a few years ago. After doing some random "raw material" sketches, I came up with my first actual concept. I was so happy with it at the time that I even spent some extra time coloring it. Now I was *really* hooked.

FIGURE 7.2   *The first concept.*

Nevertheless, I was faithful to the principle of having multiple concepts to choose from. I forced myself to try a few more options. I say "forced" because it was a struggle: my own brain was working hard against me, trying to convince me that there's no point trying because, obviously, this was already as awesome as it can be.

Figure 7.3 shows some of the other options I came up with and the final concept I ended up submitting.

| CAPTURE

CONCEPT

| VISION | PRODUCTION | PLAN

|

FIGURE 7.3 *More options.*

Now, I don't know what *you* think of these results, but for me, looking at my first concept now—in light of the other options—is quite painful. It feels outdated, lacks personality, and generally looks like a beginner's work. And yet, I wasn't able to see that until I had those other concepts to compare it with.

The first idea trap can send you heading in the wrong direction before you even properly started your project, and that's a very costly mistake. Make sure you test your concept against other options at this early stage, before you invest any serious effort in that direction.

More Pattern Breaking

Even when you are fully prepared—even eager—to try other options, getting your brain to let go of a concept it really likes can be tough. You'll often find yourself being pulled right back to that first solution, even though you're actively trying to find a new path.

Well, you already know what *that* is: it's a thinking pattern. You know how to deal with it, too: most of the methods we've discussed in the previous chapter will work here, too. Take a long break, allow yourself to be silly and wrong, and—perhaps the most effective technique for this part of the process—change your tools. With a combination of these techniques, it shouldn't be too hard to break the loop and discover new possibilities.

This is a good place to stop reading again and continue the *Exotica Animal Fashion* exercise. Gather up the raw materials you've created in step 1, put yourself in daydream mode, and see what you can come up with. If nothing clicks, try coming up with some more raw materials. If you feel confused or overwhelmed, try switching between forming concepts in your head and physically playing with the ideas you've captured.

Once you have two or three strong, exciting concepts to choose between, you can move on to the third and last step in concept stage: coming up with your final concept.

Chapter 8

Your Final Concept

We've come to the final step of the concept workflow. At this point, you ideally have two or three good concepts that have emerged organically from your heap of captured raw ideas.

Sometimes, it's very clear which concept you should go with—in which case, this last step is very simple. However, that's not always the case. You'll often find yourself excited about more than one of your concepts, and even if you do have a clear favorite, the other ones may still have a lot to offer.

If choosing between your babies is hard, being objective about it is even harder. Nevertheless, it is essential that you try to gain some objectivity and see your concepts for what they truly are. Scale matters at this point: If you're working on a small project—say, a couple of days long—the stakes aren't very high. Just go with the option that feels good to you in the moment. On a major project, however, the decision you're about to make is going to be a part of your life for a long time, and in that case, it makes sense to put some effort in choosing wisely.

Choosing Wisely

As with breaking patterns, objectivity is a matter of resetting your mind so that you can look at things in a new way.

I highly recommend taking a good, long break at this point. Depending on your schedules and the scale of the project, this could be anything between a day or two and a couple of weeks. The longer the better—just make sure it's not so long that the whole project loses momentum.

It's also a good idea is to pitch your concepts to creative friends or collogues and have a good discussion about it. The mere act of pitching will often give you a fresh point of view of your concepts. Coupled with some debate and feedback from multiple creative minds, this is a great way of gaining some perspective and objectivity.

Often, concepts will evolve and morph during these conversations. Make sure you let them. In my experience, this is a point where major breakthroughs tend to happen. You should be prepared to come out of the discussion with a concept that isn't one of those you came in with. It's going to be hard not to be protective of your original concepts, but try and give yourself permission to go with the discussion and see where it takes you. Besides, no one is taking your existing ideas away. You can always decide to discard the new option and instead go with one of your original concepts.

Final Wet Capture

Now that you have chosen your concept, there's only one thing left to do: make sure you have it properly captured. This is going to be the core of your work, and it's very important to have it anchored.

I advise you to make sure your final concept capture is more wet than dry. Because of the way these concepts are built—out of bits and pieces of different ideas—they tend to lack the clear emotional core of a holistic wet capture. Since that emotional core is exactly what you need to anchor your work to, it's not a bad idea—once you've chosen your final concept—to spend just a few minutes recapturing it with your emotion-savvy right brain.

* * *

With your concept chosen and captured, it's time to proceed to the Vision stage. Before we do that, let's look at a few safety rules for the concept stage.

Chapter 9

The Concept
Safety Rules

Always Start from Within

For many creatives, searching for ideas starts with Google. It's an easy starting point and a quick solution to the blank page problem.

To illustrate: imagine you're working on a section in a computer game that takes place in a large toy store. You fire up Google image search, type *toy store*, and get all the raw material you'll need to build your concept with.

This process is not necessarily wrong, but it wouldn't get you the most unique results. That's because it has nothing to do with *you* personally. Anybody can perform the same search and get the same results, and when you work with commonplace raw materials, you're likely to end up with a commonplace concept.

A better approach would be to start the process from within. Think of what a toy store means to you personally. What does it reminds *you* of? How does it make *you* feel? Then, break your patterns a few times and come up with even more answers.

By the time you'll do you first Google search, you'll already have an established point of view.

When I had to design a toy store for one of my project, I did exactly that. I asked myself: when I was a kid, how did it feel to be in a toy store? One of the answers I gave myself was, "It was like being in Aladdin's cave: full of precious wonders that I can't have." Figure 9.1 is my capture of that thought.

FIGURE 9.1   Toy store as Aladdin's cave.

I did eventually search for "toy store" images, but it was after the expressive concept was already chosen, and I was able to fuse the information into my existing point of view. If the first thing I had done was to search toy store images online, I probably wouldn't have thought of the cave idea at all. The factual nature of the photos would have led me down a more matter-of-fact path, and I would have ended up with a less expressive concept.

The safety rule: Listen to your unique inner voice first. Start your search for ideas inside your head, not outside of it.

CAPTURE | CONCEPT | VISION | PRODUCTION | PLAN

Don't Overdo It

At one company I worked for, the design team worked on a female character who was quite secondary in the story. They decided to try all sorts of hairstyles and ended up designing around 20 different options. There was a whole wall covered with nothing but hairstyles for this character.

The design team had so many options in front of them that they got seriously confused. They debated and argued about that design for a long time, not being able to decide what to go with and delaying the entire production. After a few weeks, having lost all chance of objectivity, they finally made a choice—and it was terrible (they ended up going back and changing it later).

When you come up with too many concepts, two things happen. First, you get confused because there are too many good options. Second, it creates a psychological need to justify all the time you've invested in these options. That means choosing right becomes super important, which means you need to invest more time in choosing, which means it gets even *more* crucial—and now you're stuck in a loop of confusion, time wasting, and fear of failure.

The safety rule: Don't come up with too many competing concepts. Two or three good options are quite enough in most cases.

Choose, Don't Mix

We tend to care about our ideas more than most of us would be willing to admit. Letting go of a good one can be harder than you expect. When you have several good concepts to choose from, it can be tempting to try and combine them, so that no good idea goes to waste.

That urge, however natural, is dangerous.

The most common mixing mistake is what I call the "Frankenstein concept": a concept made of bits and piece of your original concepts. This approach rarely works: you can't make a beautiful thing by gluing together pieces of several beautiful things (Figure 9.2A).

Another version is the "compromised concept," which aims to hit a middle point between two (or more) strong concepts. By definition, the result is going to be a mediocre concept, resulting in a poorly defined piece (Figure 9.2B).

Finally, there's the "crammed together" solution, in which you don't choose at all but use two concepts together in the same piece. This is guaranteed to get you an overloaded and confusing piece (Figure 9.2C).

Concept #1   Concept #2   A   B   C

FIGURE 9.2 *Two strong, clear concepts get (A) Frankensteined, (B) compromised, and (C) crammed together. In each case, the result is vague and/or confusing. Forcing strong concepts to live together is almost always a bad idea.*

Whichever way you look at it, forcing strong concepts to live together is almost always a bad idea. It's like trying to simultaneously get to two different destinations, with only one car.

Let me stress that none of this relates to step 2 of the process, which we've discussed in Chapter 7. In that part of the process, fusing together ideas was what it was all about. Once your ideas have fused together to strong concepts, however, Lego time is over. Forcing strong concepts to live together will only diminish them.

The safety rule: Don't mix your concepts—make a choice! You must get used to letting go of good ideas.

CAPTURE | CONCEPT | VISION | PRODUCTION | PLAN

Conclusion

This concludes the concept part of the creative workflow.

You now have a reliable workflow to get you all the way from the blank page to an exciting concept—every time, on demand. Instead of looking for ready-made concepts, you're now looking for raw, incomplete, weird, or even random ideas, out of which great concepts are going to emerge. You're no longer relying on inspiration for your ideas: your ideas are going to create the inspiration, not the other way around.

You've learned to work from the inside out, building on your personal experiences and associations as your primary source of ideas, and you have at your disposal several techniques for successively breaking your thinking patterns and extracting precious mental gems from the deepest corridors of you mind. Thus, your concepts are going to be fresher and more exciting than ever, giving a strong core and a unique voice to your work.

Remember that the concept part of the process is all about keeping it light and playful. The concept stage is not about being a craftsman; it's about having *fun*, like a child building dreams out of Legos.

For the child, playing is where it both starts and ends; for the professional creative, this is only the beginning. In the next part of the workflow, you'll transition into a very different thinking mode. You'll slow down, delve deep into your concept, and develop it into a full creative vision.

AT A GLANCE:

THE CONCEPT

From the blank page
to an exciting core idea

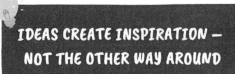

IDEAS CREATE INSPIRATION —
NOT THE OTHER WAY AROUND

IDEAS   CONCEPT

THE CONCEPT WORKFLOW

STEP 1 — COME UP WITH PLENTY OF RANDOM IDEAS
STEP 2 — FORM A FEW VIABLE CONCEPTS
STEP 3 — CHOOSE & CAPTURE THE FINAL CONCEPT

BREAKING PATTERNS

- TAKE A BREAK
- CHANGE YOUR TOOLS
- GET SILLY
- EXTERNAL PATTERN BREAKERS
- BRAINSTORMING WITH OTHERS

THE SAFTEY RULES

- START FROM WITHIN
- DON'T OVERDO IT
- CHOOSE, DON'T MIX

THE VISION

From Raw Concept
to Solid Vision

"Give me six hours to chop down a tree, and I will spend the first four sharpening the axe."

Abraham Lincoln

Chapter 10

The Gap

So you have a strong and exciting concept for your work. Great! That means you know what you're going to make. But are you ready to start making it?

Not a Walk in the Park

We all start our journey as makers with short, spontaneous creative bursts. No one starts out writing a 500-page novel or making a feature film. We write a short story, make a drawing of our favorite action hero, come up with a little song to play for our friends—that's the sort of work we all begin with. Even when we start taking it more seriously, gathering knowledge and practicing our craft, most of our creations take only a few hours to complete.

This kind of casual creative work is like going for a walk in the park. You have some free time and the weather is nice, so you put your shoes on and head out. You know you're going to the park, but you don't have to decide which particular path you're going to take, what bench you'll sit on, and for how long.

CAPTURE | CONCEPT | VISION | PRODUCTION | PLAN

As you start transitioning from an amateur creative to a professional, the scope of your work grows. It gets more ambitious, more demanding. You start venturing further and further away from the comfort zone of what comes easy. It takes longer, too: a single project may take weeks or even months to complete.

This kind of creative work is no longer a walk in the park. This is much closer to going for a long hike in, say, the Himalayas. It requires a completely different mindset, and here's why: because there is a *gap* between the point at which you decide you're going to the Himalayas, and the moment you're putting on your shoes and start walking. For a journey like that, you'll want to invest some time in preparation. You'll read about the hike, watch videos, and look at maps. You'll decide in advance exactly what route you're going to take, and where you'll stop for the night. You might even do a few preliminary short trips before you take on the big one—just to get used to the environment and its challenges. In short, you'll want to have a very clear idea of what your hike is going to be like, long before you ever set foot on the actual trail.

The exact same logic applies when you go into a creative project that's going to take more than a few hours to complete. There's a *gap* between knowing where you're going—that's your concept—and the point at which you're ready to produce the actual work. Here, too, you'll want to know everything you *can* know about the work, so that you have a very clear picture of what the end result is going to be like before you start working on it.

That clear mental preview of your work is your creative *vision*.

A Good Investment

Sounds obvious, doesn't it? And yet, many creatives are not fully aware of just how important having a solid creative vision is. The very idea of spending a significant amount of time *not* doing the actual work but preparing for it can be difficult to digest.

Case in point: some years ago, I worked at a small animation studio on a low-budget game project. The schedules were quite tight (I believe we had to finish our part in about two weeks). What's more, the animation style was new to us. So, once I agreed with my supervisor on what we're going to do (the concept), I decided to invest some time in preparing for it.

Three days into the project, with the rest of the animators already deep into animating their parts, I was still just playing around, exploring and experimenting. My supervisor called me aside. "Dude, what are you doing? We don't have time for this. You've just wasted three whole days producing nothing." I tried to explain why I was doing it, but I could see I wasn't getting through. We agreed I'd start animating "for real" the next day—which, fortunately, was my plan anyway.

By now, my vision was crystal clear, and I zoomed right through the work with zero complications. That was not true for the other animators: they were struggling with the unfamiliar style, often getting stuck and having to erase and redo entire sections. Since I had everything worked out in advance, I didn't have any of these problems. I ended up beating the deadline by a couple of days and helping others finish their work on time.

In case you were wondering: the supervisor in that story wasn't some incompetent amateur. In fact, he is one of the smartest, most experienced, and most talented people I have ever worked with. And yet, he was obviously missing something important about the workflow: that the time we put in developing a strong vision is not time wasted. It is time *invested*, since it creates more time down the road.

A Driving Force

Saving time and meeting deadlines is great, but creative vision is about something much greater than that. I won't try to put it into words; someone already did that far better than I can. The following quote comes from one of the greatest artists of all time, the man who sculpted the famous David and created the ceiling murals of the Sistine Chapel. This is how Michelangelo Buonarroti explains vision:

In every block of marble, I see a statue; as plain as though it stood before me, shaped and perfect in attitude and action. I have only to hew away the rough walls that imprison the lovely apparition to reveal it to the other eyes as mine see it.

What Michelangelo articulates with such eloquence is that having a strong creative vision changes the entire experience of creating something. It isn't just "work" anymore. It becomes a mission— an internal need to show the world something that, at this point, only you can see. That's a powerful driving force that's going to give you the energy and motivation you'll need to see the project through.

The Missing Quote

I know what many of you must be thinking right now. "Well that's all fine and great if you're a genius like Michelangelo was, but what if I'm not? What if I *can't* look at a block of marble and see a statue 'as plain as though it stood before me'? What if I *can't* see a finished painting on my canvas, or a finished website on my blank browser page? What then?"

Let me tell you a secret: even for the great Michelangelo, that "lovely apparition" did not materialize out of thin air. We know this because we have his preparation work to look at. His quote, beautiful as it is, leaves out something critical: the *process* (Figure 10.1). Coming up with a compelling vision requires time and effort. Like the concept, it's not supposed to just be there for you. You need to create it.

CAPTURE — CONCEPT — **VISION** — PRODUCTION — PLAN

FIGURE 10.1   *Michelangelo's studies for Libyan Sibyl (one of the famous Sistine Chapel murals). He might have been able to clearly see the painting on the wall before painting it, but it did take a fair amount of work—even for him.*

In the next chapter, we'll look into the process of developing your raw concept into a rich and solid vision.

Chapter 11

The Study

The study is how you develop your raw concept into a full vision. We're going to discuss two different ways of studying a subject: *the dry study* and *the wet study*. These, of course, relate to the bigger issue of left-brain thinking and right-brain thinking; but we'll get to that later.

Let's start with a concrete example.

AppSpace was a mobile app I created for Android phones. For the main screen, I needed to design an image containing as many items as possible for the users to click on: a camera, a calendar, a notepad, and so on. The concept I landed on for this image was the cartoony home office from the 1980s shown in Figure 11.1.

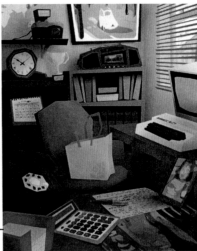

FIGURE 11.1   1980s room concept (left) vs. the final result (right).

This gave me a clear direction, but not much else. It wasn't the kind of thing I was used to doing, which meant I wasn't able to imagine my final image very clearly. It wasn't even the angle or the composition I wanted. My creative vision was blurry at best; had I started producing the drawing based on that raw concept alone, I'd be setting myself up for failure.

The Dry Study

Dry studying means expanding and clarifying your vision by collecting (or creating) as much helpful information about it as you can. In our Himalayan hike metaphor, this would be akin to learning everything you can about the Himalayas: reading about it, looking at maps, charting possible routes, and so on.

For AppSpace, my first step in developing a more solid vision was to come up with as many ideas as possible for the kind of items a 1980s room would contain. I captured a bunch of props ideas from my own memory (being a 1980s kid myself), then googled lots more. Figure 11.2 shows one of my sketch

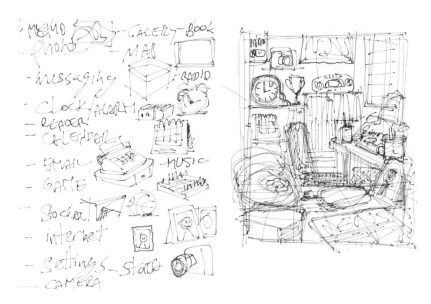

FIGURE 11.2   *Dry-studying possible props for the 1980s room.*

pages, coupled with a very rough sketch capturing a possible composition for the final frame. Notice that, while the core concept (cartoony 80's room) did not change, the study did heavily influence the presentation of the concept (the frame's composition).

This was helpful in terms of the objects that the room might contain, but I was also unclear regarding the visual style, the lighting, and the technique I'd be using. I explored those areas by looking through many photos and illustrations, capturing or saving the ones that felt relevant.

My dry study for the 1980s room didn't take too long—perhaps a couple of hours or so. In other projects, the dry study stage could be a lot more substantial. JK Rowling famously studied the Harry Potter world for years before starting to actually write the books. A documentary by A&E shows her pulling out a large box containing hundreds of notes, maps, sketches, family trees, and all sorts of other information that helped her make Harry Potter's world rich and unique. Writing the book, she said in the documentary, was like sculpting a story out of her mass of notes and ideas. Obviously, the box of notes was to her what the block of marble was to Michelangelo.

Collecting Captures

In the 1980s room example, notice I hadn't just collected images of the props. Instead, I *captured* those options using quick sketches and notes. Capturing may take a bit longer than saving an image or copy/pasting a piece of text, but it has a few major advantages:

It sticks. Have you ever noticed how, when you're writing a reminder to yourself, you tend to remember it a lot better—even without ever looking at the note again? That's because the very act of capturing imprints the thought more strongly in your brain. In the same way, when you capture your dry-study materials instead of just collecting them, you make them "stick." That'll make them more accessible to you, if and when you'll need to use them on the fly during the Production process.

You use only what matters. As we know, a capture is a summary of what's important to you in a subject. By capturing it, you get to extract from the reference material only what's relevant to your work. If and when you'll want to use the item in your work, it'll be easier to fit it in.

You have the freedom to modify. Capturing an item rather than simply collecting it gives you the freedom to adjust it to your project's needs.

Ownership. Capturing the reference materials gives you a sense of ownership over the ingredients that go into your vision. That means you're creating a stronger emotional connection with your budding vision, and that's important.

CAPTURE | CONCEPT | VISION | PRODUCTION | PLAN

More Raw Materials

If dry studying reminds you of the "raw materials" process described in the concept stage, you're not wrong. That's because the principle is similar: you don't expect something amazing to just be there for you. Instead, you come up with many random and insignificant options, and put your trust in the idea that cooking with great ingredients will produce a delicious meal.

The same pattern breakers we've discussed in the previous section are also going to be helpful for the dry study. In this stage of the workflow, I tend to lean more heavily on external information—searching the Internet and coming up with interesting and unexpected ideas. Getting silly is less relevant for this stage, but taking breaks, changing your tools, and involving other people will still be helpful in creating the amount of raw materials you need for a solid and rich vision.

Let's summarize: The dry study gives you a wealth of raw materials to use in your vision (and later, your work). It's like acquiring a rich vocabulary, allowing you to express yourself in unique and interesting ways. You also get more flexible: if one solution doesn't work as expected, you have plenty of alternatives at your disposal. This can come in handy when dealing with sudden changes, unexpected snags, and creative blocks.

Now let's turn to the other side of the coin and see what the wet study has to offer.

The Wet Study

When stage performers—actors, musician, dancers, etc.—go on stage, they experience a lot of stress. Few of us are completely immune to stage fright, and even seasoned performers

CAPTURE | CONCEPT | VISION | PRODUCTION | PLAN

say they experience it on regular basis. The stress can seriously interfere with a performance: anyone who was ever on stage knows how difficult it is to do your very best in front of an audience.

We all know how performers deal with that challenge: they *rehearse*. They take the time and do it again and again and again and *again* until they can perform the part without thinking about it. Only then can they hope to give a truly great performance.

Why am I talking about stage performers?

Because every creative project that's meant to be seen by someone has something of a stage performance in it. When we're in front of our canvas, computer screen, or piece of clay, somewhere at the back of our minds, we're constantly aware of our invisible audience (Figure 11.3). We're eager to impress, and at the same time, we're afraid we'll fail and look stupid. And it's not only the crowd we're aware of: it's also our peers, our critics, and our bosses. I noticed that while I work, I often imagine specific people praising or rebuking my work. Many creatives I talked to confessed of having similar thoughts.

FIGURE 11.3   *The Production stage can often feel like you're "on stage."*

I'm not saying that our creative stage fright is anywhere near as strong as that of stage performers. But it does come from the same place, and therefore, it makes sense for us to use the same kind of solution.

So, think of *the wet study* as a form of rehearsal: you spend time doing work that you've decided in advance never to show anyone. That gives you a chance to relax and lower your creative guards: no one's watching now. You're free to spend quality time with your work, get to know it, practice it, experiment with it, and get more comfortable with it. In our hiking metaphor, this would be akin to going on a few shorter hikes around the Himalayas before taking on the "real" one.

Wet exploration is an excellent way of simplifying complex problems by coping with one thing at a time. You can target specific aspects or elements of your work, practice them individually, identify potential difficulties, and find solutions upfront. Once you feel comfortable with the various parts of your work, it's easier to combine everything together without the stress and without stumbling over yourself.

Another great benefit of the wet study is that it provides you with a safe space to try things out. In that safe space, away from your audience, you can allow yourself to be spectacularly wrong. You can make bold choices, try unlikely solutions, get silly, and let happy accidents happen. What doesn't work, you don't have to use; no one will ever know. What does work, you get to keep and use in the Production stage.

In my 1980s room example, once I was done with the dry study, I spent some time experimenting. I did a few throwaway item designs to nail the style, a couple of quick lighting tests, and came up with a couple of technical solutions in the process. As you can see in Figure 11.4, these tests are not fully developed artwork; they are super-quick captures, completely focused on those specific aspects. The whole thing took just a few hours.

CAPTURE | CONCEPT | VISION | PRODUCTION | PLAN

FIGURE 11.4 **1980s room wet study.**

An UnFortunate Event

The dry study makes sense to people. "Learn more about my project? Sure, good idea." The wet study, I find, is harder to swallow: "Spend hours or even days doing throwaway work? With an already tough deadline to meet? You've got to be kidding me".

I already told you about the misunderstanding with my animation supervisor. Let me tell you another story, this time about an unfortunate event that taught me a valuable lesson about throwaway work.

This was another gaming project. I had an urgent task that *had* to be finished by the end of the day, and there was still a lot of work to be done. I got to work very early—before 7:00 a.m.—and worked in a frenzy. Four hours later—at around 11:00—disaster hit: the software crashed while I was saving my work, the file got corrupted, and I could no longer open it. It was unrecoverable. Just like that, my entire morning of hard work went down the drain. I had nothing.

The first thing I did, of course, was panic and throw a tantrum. Once that was out of the way, I settled down and tried to figure out what to do next. What *was* there to do? I had to submit *something* that evening, even if I didn't have time to do it well. So, I got back to work, starting from scratch.

Just one hour later, I was shocked to realize I'd gotten further than where I left off. Somehow, this one hour had been more productive than the four hours before—and remember, these were four hours of my hardest, most focused efforts! What's more, the quality of my work wasn't harmed at all. If anything, it was now better than what I had before the crash.

What happened here?

Well, think of it this way: how much time does it take to write book? A lot—often, many years. How long would it take to retype the same book, word for word? A few days, probably. Why? Because, physically writing the words—or putting paint on canvas, or animating a CG puppet around, or manipulating vectors in a design software—doesn't actually take that long. In a creative project, most of the time is spent thinking, trying stuff, erasing, making mistakes, and going back to fix the mess.

That process of trial and error took up most of my time between 7:00 and 11:00 that day, before the software crashed.

Between 11:00 and 12:00, it was a completely different kind of work. Sure, I had to physically redo the animation, but the thinking and trying and choosing and fixing were already done. Both the process and the result were vivid in my mind; in other words, I had a strong *vision*. Though I didn't realize it at the time, the four hours of lost work served as a much-too-long wet study.

You may be asking yourself how come the *quality* was better the second time around. That's because the vision in my head was so complete—to the last detail—that I was able to let the work flow out naturally. I easily avoided the problems that distracted and confused me in the first round. Since trial and error weren't a part of it, I worked a lot cleaner and was spared the fuss of cleaning up traces of old mistakes.

Here's the kicker: because my work was clean and straightforward instead of a patched-up mess, the work that *followed* this one-hour effort was *also* made faster. So, because I had lost four hours of work, I ended up finishing *earlier* than I had expected, and with a result that was probably better than it would otherwise have been (Figures 11.5 and 11.6).

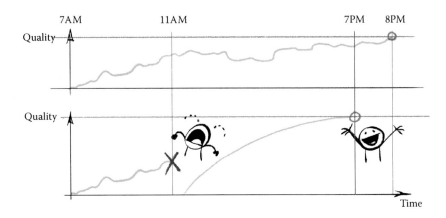

FIGURE 11.5 *Top: how it would have gone if it wasn't for the technical meltdown. Bottom: how it actually went. The result ended up being better— something I would not have believed if it hadn't happened to me.*

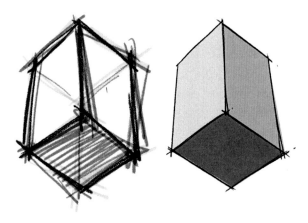

FIGURE 11.6 *Here's a visualization of the same idea. Suppose you don't have the kind of skill it takes to draw box B right off the bat. Which method would be faster: (1) trying to do it anyway, constantly erasing your mistakes while trying to get it right and clean at the same time? Or (2) doing the trial-and-error in wet-exploration mode first (box A) and then drawing box B from scratch without having to clean anything?*

Feeding Your Brain

We've looked at two different ways of developing your raw concept into a full vision: the dry study, which is all about collecting information, and the wet study, which is about rehearsing your work. How does that relate to dry and wet captures and the idea of the logical left brain vs. the intuitive right brain?

Think about it this way: suppose you wanted to learn as much as you could about a person in a short space of time. One way to do that would be to get some hard information about them: their work resume, where they're from, their income, what hobbies they have, and so on. This feeds your left brain: based on the hard information, it can make some logical assumptions about what that person might be like.

The other way, of course, is to just spend some time with them. It won't give you any hard data about them, but it will give you plenty of information—subtle, holistic, unquantifiable information that will help you develop some intuition about that person. In other words, information that feeds your right brain.

Dry and wet explorations do exactly the same thing. Collecting information about your work helps your left brain form a strong creative vision based on reason. Rehearsing your work helps your right brain form a strong creative vision based on intuition. Together, they help you form a vivid and well-rounded vision, just like Michelangelo's marble apparition; the kind of vision that's going to carry you through the Production stage with clarity, confidence, and motivation (Figure 11.7).

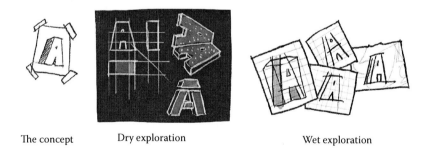

The concept   Dry exploration   Wet exploration

FIGURE 11.7 *Dry vs. wet study. Collecting information about your work helps your left brain form a creative vision based on reason. Rehearsing your work helps your right brain form a creative vision based on intuition.*

There's only one thing left to do before plunging forward and producing your actual work. That last step in your preparation process is the heart and soul of the creative workflow. I call it *the premake.*

Chapter 12

The Premake

We now come to a crucial step in the creative workflow. It has many names: in architecture, they call it a *scale model*; in music, a *demo*; in film, *animatic*; in game design, *mockup*; in web design, *wireframe*; in writing, *an outline*. The names are different, but the principle is always the same: *before you go into the Production process of a major project, you must capture your vision of it*. I call this capture *the premake*, and it's the most important capture in the entire process (Figure 12.1).

Think of it this way: every significant creative work that takes longer than a few hours to complete should be made twice. First you premake it, then you make it.

In the following pages, I'll discuss some of the reasons the premake is such a central creativity tool and what to keep in mind when you premake.

CAPTURE | CONCEPT | VISION | PRODUCTION | PLAN

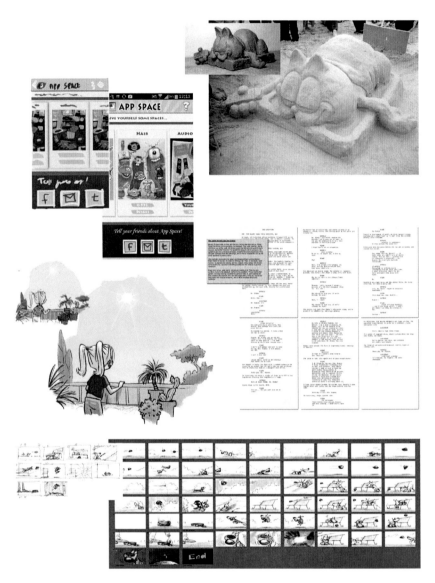

FIGURE 12.1 *First you premake it, then you make it. No matter what creative field you're working in, the principle is always the same: before you go into the Production process of a major project, you must capture your vision. Clockwise from the top, premakes vs. final work in: sculpting (maquette), screenwriting (synopsis), storyboarding (thumbnails), illustration (sketch), UI design (mockup).*

A Unique Vantage Point

In most projects, the Production stage is by far the longest and most demanding part of the work. As a ballpark figure, in a typical project done by a single person or a very small group, the ratio is 75% for the Production and only 25% for everything that comes before it. In larger projects, that ratio can be much more dramatic: the Production stage may take 90% of the budget or more, since that's the part involving large teams (Concept and Vision are usually done by relatively small teams).

That means that the premake comes at a unique point in the creative workflow. It's a point at which you already have a clear and detailed view of the end result, and yet you've invested only a fraction of your total resources in the project. This makes it the best moment to capture and test your ideas (Figure 12.2).

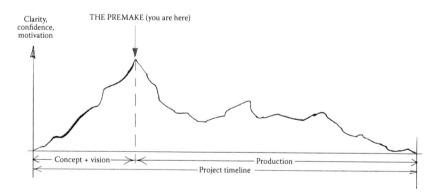

FIGURE 12.2   *The premake captures your vision at a unique point in the process: you already have a clear view of the finished work but have invested only a fraction of your total resources in it. It's the apex of clarity, confidence, and excitement in the timeline of your project.*

Why Should You Test Your Vision?

If you can see the end result so clearly in your mind's eye, why should you need to test it?

Have you ever had a brilliant shower idea, and then when you rushed out all dripping to capture it, it suddenly seemed rather lame? I've had that happen to me many times. I've also experienced the opposite: capturing an idea that feels weird initially and finding that it's actually working rather well.

The point is that, a vision that's locked inside your head is hard to judge objectively. Once you capture it—even very crudely—you get to see it much more clearly. You also get to show it to other people and get their feedback on it. You even get to put your capture into the context in which your work is going to appear, which is a huge advantage (we'll talk more about the influence of context in Chapter 23).

Case in point: for AppSpace (my mobile app), once we developed a clear vision of it, we were able to knock up a crude working premake in just a couple of days. We did this by using temporary artwork and focusing on the basic functionality. We then tested our vision by letting people try it out, watching them using it, and listening to their feedback. We got some great positive feedback, but we were surprised by how difficult it was for some people to figure out how to use the app. As a result, we made a few important changes to the app and even added a quick "getting started" guide. As you can imagine, we were very pleased to be able to make those fundamental changes before any real hard work has been done.

When it comes to showing your work and receiving feedback, the premake actually has a certain advantage over a more detailed version. You'd be surprised at how often people focus their feedback on the most negligible aspects of your work. This happens even with experienced professionals, let alone laymen. When you show a premake, you bypass that problem: because it only contains what's really important in the work, the feedback you'll get will be much more on point.

Thus, the main function of the premake is to give you *confidence*. Since you've looked at your vision with a critical eye, shown it to people, tested it in its context, and modified it according to your conclusions, you can confidently put everything you've got into the work knowing you're not likely to end up realizing it was all just a big mistake.

An Anchor for Your Vision

Testing your vision is super important, but the Premake has an even more important role in the process: anchoring your vision. What do I mean by that?

The mind is a dynamic thing. It changes all the time: a new experience, a story someone tells you, a family feud, even the passage of time itself—all these constantly reshape your perception. One thing's certain: it's not a safe place to hold something in for the long-term. That clear and solid vision you have in your head right now can easily morph into something entirely different in a matter of days or hours, without you even noticing. This could be destructive to your work.

By capturing your vision as a premake, you anchor your vision to a fixed point and keep it from floating away in a random direction. That doesn't mean you can't make changes if you really need to; it just means you're in control of whether a change happens or not. As you'll see in the next section, a successful Production process is very much dependent on having that stable point of reference.

A Message to Your Future Self

We already know that a good vision needs to be rich with details and ideas. Unfortunately, that wealth of details can also be overwhelming, and it gets even more so in the Production stage. Exciting new ideas are going to keep popping up along the way, tempting you to follow them and see where they might lead. In a long production stage, it's not at all rare to find yourself completely lost.

By boiling your vision down to its essentials, the premake helps you stay on the right path throughout the project. It sends a clear message to the future overwhelmed you: "remember *this*? This is what's truly important about this project. As long as you focus your efforts on *this*, you're going to be okay" (Figure 12.3).

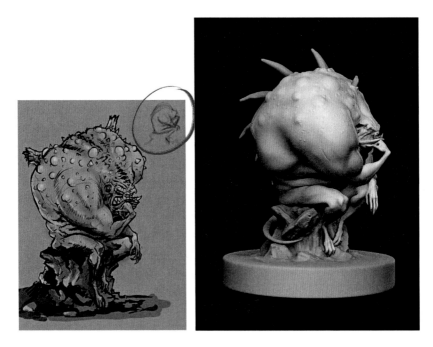

FIGURE 12.3 *The vision you hold in your head may include many inconsequential details, which will change as the work evolves (e.g., the shape of the spikes on the creature's back). The premake helps you clearly state what shouldn't change: the conceptual core (marked red). (Artwork courtesy of Rafi Ben Aharon.)*

Your Most Important Communication Tool

If you're leading a team of creatives, the premake will help you ensure that everyone's on the same page and that your team has a good grasp on what's important to you.

A while ago, I worked in a medium-sized studio, employing about 150–200 creatives. I was part of a team drawing the storyboards on a film that, unfortunately, had no clear premake. To be precise, there *used* to be a premake, but over time the script and the directors' vision changed. No one bothered making an updated premake, so at this point, we were freestyling it.

About a year into the project, we were having lunch with the directors. As we discussed the film, it suddenly became clear that the two directors didn't agree on what the essential message of the film was. What's worse, until that moment, they weren't even aware that they disagreed. I came out of that lunch with the sinking sensation that the film was never going to be made. Sure enough, about two months later, the film collapsed and the studio was shut down.

I have no doubt that a good premake would have prevented that misunderstanding—or at least revealed it *much* sooner, when it was still easy to manage.

The premake is an important communication tool, not only for leads but also when you're part of a team working in parallel on different parts of a project. Your premakes can help others in the team see where you're going with your part of the work, long before you finish creating it. They'll be able to respond to your vision in *their* work, and you'll be able to respond to their vision in your work. This kind of vision-level communication helps prevent frustrating mistakes, and fuses together the various parts of the work.

In the end, creative collaboration is all about communication—and whatever your role is, the premake is your most important communication tool.

What Makes a Good Premake?

Now that we know what premaking is good for, let's try to outline the kind of premake that would achieve those results. In other words: what makes a good premake?

Fast

The more time you invest in the premake, the more your vision will morph even as you capture it. You're really racing against time, which is why I always aim to create my premake in two hours or less. I call it "the two hours rule". In my experience, if you can't premake your work in two hours or less, you probably don't have a clear enough vision of it, and if that's the case, you should go back to developing and clarifying your vision before moving on.

Why two hours? Simply because this is the amount of time an average creative can stay focused without having to take a break.

It's worth mentioning here that very large projects often have premakes that are themselves major projects, taking much more than two hours. In fact, some premakes take months or even years to complete. However, when a premake becomes a significant project in and of itself, *that* project needs a premake too, and at the end of that chain of premakes, there should always be a crisp two-hour premake that captures the heart of the core of the essence of the entire project. We will look into the idea of projects-within-projects again when we discuss managing your workflow in Section VI.

Cheap

In addition to being fast, a good premake would require minimal investment of resources—whether it's budget, materials, or manpower. Since one of the main purposes of premaking is to test your vision and get feedback, there's no sense in investing too much in it; chances are, it's going to change a bit anyway.

Having a cheap premake also helps you avoid the *sunk cost fallacy* I've mentioned before: the psychological effect that makes you unable to see the flaws in something you've invested a lot in.

Easy to Take In

I know you're proud of your craft (and you should be: you've worked hard to acquire those skills), but for your premake, try to focus on simplicity and clarity. Complex structures and ideas, difficult language, challenging technology—all these will make it harder for people to give you the kind of feedback you need.

CAPTURE — CONCEPT — VISION — PRODUCTION — PLAN

If you can, try to create a premake that your "feedback audience" can grasp and comment on within minutes, or even seconds. If you need to sacrifice accuracy for simplicity, that's okay. The premake is a communication tool and therefore should be easily accessible.

For that matter, remember that the premake is also a tool for yourself—in the Production stage, you're going to refer to it often in order to keep yourself focused and on track. For that to happen, you need to be able to take in the Premake almost at a glance. If you have to read five pages or watch a 15-minute video every time you want to check your premake, I can guarantee you that you won't—which can be seriously bad for your work going forward.

Bottom line: always go for clarity and brevity, not for show. A small, simple premake is the kind of premake you want.

* * *

The premake represents the apex of clarity, confidence, and excitement in the timeline of your project. Everything that comes before it leads up to it, and everything that comes after it refers to it. With that done, you're finally ready to start the Production stage.

Before we begin, let's quickly discuss a few safety rules for the Vision stage.

13

The Vision
Safety Rules

Always Set a Timeframe

When you get used to the idea of doing studies before the Production stage, it can become somewhat addictive. Here you are, playing around, learning stuff, geeking out, not committing to anything. It's fun, and its guilt-free: you're technically working, aren't you? It's not hard to see how the useful idea of developing your vision can become a form of procrastination. To avoid this problem, I strongly suggest that you decide up front on a specific amount of time you're going to take for studying.

How much time should that be? Well, the answer obviously depends on many factors, but here's a ballpark answer I have found to work well in small- and medium-scale projects.

If you're reasonably familiar with the landscape of your project—the kind of content, the technology, the client, the team—then spending about 20% of the allotted project time in studying should be enough. If you need to, you can probably do with less.

If, on the other hand, you're *not* familiar with the landscape of the project—if you truly are looking at a long hike in a foreign land—I wouldn't dare go into Production before spending at least 25%–35% of the time in dry and wet studies. In extreme situations, even 50% is not too much.

This, by the way, can be hard advice to follow: it means that the *less* confident you are, the *more* time you'll need to spend on throwaway work. You'll just need to toughen up and go against the natural instinct of skipping preparation and getting to work. Remember my software crash story: you'll be much better off with less time for Production but having a clear vision than with more time in Production but having a blurry vision (Figure 13.1).

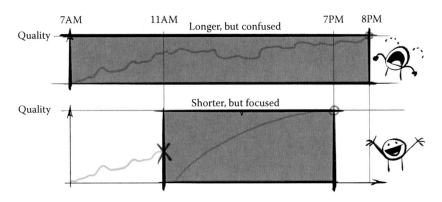

FIGURE 13.1 *Shorter vs. longer. You'll get less anxiety and a better result with a focused shorter Production stage than with a longer confused one.*

The safety rule: don't let your study become procrastination. Before starting, set a specific time frame that reflects your familiarity with the project.

"If It Comes Out Okay, Maybe We'll Use It"

A very common pitfall—especially when you have a tight budget or a tough deadline—is to want to use some of the work you've been doing in the wet study stage for the work itself. Why not? If it comes out okay, why not use it?

Here's what usually ends up happening: instead of genuinely taking the pressure off and allowing yourself a safe space to experiment, there's now going to be a voice at the back of your brain saying that you *might* be on stage right now after all; perhaps, there *is* an invisible audience to this work. That, of course, defeats the whole purpose of the wet study.

Case in point: a student of mine was working on a personal animation project in which she was going to use a technique she had never tried before. She was smart about it, deciding to animate a few seconds as a wet study—just to get herself more familiar with the new technique.

It started out great: her work was rough but fresh and inspiring. Then she looked at the calendar and the looming deadline and got anxious. Since this was going so nicely, she thought, she might be able to use some of these tests in the actual film.

The effect of that idea on her results was immediate and striking. Her work became constrained, she started tinkering with insignificant details, things started to drag on, and suddenly she was feeling confused and frustrated.

When I realized what was happening, I insisted on her doing the wet study with dummy elements, so that it wouldn't be possible to use it in the actual work. As soon as she switched to that, the work started to flow as before.

The safety rule: don't mix your creative modes. Study when you study, produce when you produce.

Juice Up the Mundane

Imagine you're working on an adaptation for *Superman*. Which part should you study more thoroughly: *The Fortress of Solitude* or *The Daily Planet* offices?

Most creatives will be drawn to studying the exciting parts and neglect the "boring" stuff in between. I guess that's natural, but if you think about it, shouldn't it be the other way around? The exciting stuff is probably the most established part of your vision; you

CAPTURE — CONCEPT — VISION — PRODUCTION — PLAN

already know a lot about it. Plus, it's already exciting! You want your audience engaged in every part of your work, and oftentimes, it's the more mundane parts of the work that could use some more juice.

Have you ever looked at something unremarkable for so long that you found yourself getting more and more attracted to it? If you haven't tried it, I highly recommend the experience. Try it now: find a mundane object around you and look at it for a good long while. If you're anything like me, you'll start noticing funky little details, and slowly, that "boring" object will become more and more intriguing to you. Clever stand-up comedians have made successful careers out of looking long and hard at mundane things in life and pointing them out in an interesting way. Audiences love that.

In Pixar's *The Incredibles*, there are of course many exciting action scenes. To me, that's not what makes the film special; many superhero films have cool action moments. What makes this film stand out—at least in my opinion—is the fact that the scenes that *could* have been boring—the suburbia parts—are just as entertaining as the naturally interesting parts.

The safety rule: don't neglect the more mundane areas of your work. With a good bit of studying, you can make them just as captivating as the exciting parts.

Don't Pass on Challenging Your Premake

We've discussed the benefits of putting your premake in context, showing it around, and getting some feedback. Surprisingly, creatives often dismiss this idea and even actively resist it. Many of us, it seems, tend to recoil from challenging our vision. Why?

Here are some of the reasons I've heard:

I'm not sure it works. This is a strange excuse. What better reason to show and discuss your premake? Do you really want to plow forward with something you feel insecure about?

I know it's good and I don't need anyone's approval. If you take that position, you're putting yourself at a lot of risk. Somehow, creatives don't always appreciate just how differently things can feel when put in context, and how biased their own judgment can be. In my experience, mature and confident creatives tend to show their work as often as possible and keep themselves attentive to feedback.

It's too rough—they won't get it. Because the premake is a crude capture, creatives are often worried that they'll be misunderstood and judged on the craft rather than the ideas they're presenting. There's a simple solution to that. All you have to do is say, "Hey, this is just a quick and rough representation of my vision. Don't mind the level of craftsmanship, just tell me what you think of the ideas." It's *that* simple. If you've done a good job capturing your vision, and if you explain exactly what it is you're showing and what kind of feedback you're looking for, people usually get it. I haven't met many people—including noncreatives—who couldn't understand a clear capture that was presented properly.

I don't have time to change anything anyway. That could be true, but information is always a good thing—even if you end up deciding not to act on it. The feedback you'll get may still come in handy during the upcoming production stage. Remember also that having a vision you're confident about is the key to an effective production stage. For that reason, a sobering piece of feedback may be worth acting on even when facing a tough deadline.

Here's the bottom line: there's no reasonable excuse to avoid feedback. Put your premake in context, show it to clever people who can articulate what they feel about the ideas, explain what a premake is and what kind of feedback you're interested in, and keep yourself open to that feedback. You'll be happy you did.

The safety rule: always challenge your vision before going into the Production stage.

Conclusion

We've discussed the gap between having a raw *concept* and having a full *vision* of the kind Michelangelo was talking about: a vivid mental preview of your final work. That's the kind of creative vision that turns a project from just a task to a personal mission: to show the world something beautiful that at present only you can see. Your vision will not only protect you from confusion but also propel you forward and give you the kind of motivation you need to carry you through the Production stage. In that sense, your vision is both your engine and your navigation system.

Unfortunately, of the three stages of the process—Concept, Vision, and Production—the Vision part is the least intuitively understood. It's obvious you need an idea; it's obvious you need to make it. Spending time doing throwaway work? Not obvious at all.

On the positive side, this gives you a real edge. You now have a clear understanding of something many of your peers don't get and which takes most creatives many years to come to grips with. If you diligently invest time developing your creative vision, despite internal and external pressures to rush to production, and if you make sure you capture your vision and challenge it, and then respond to the feedback you get - you'll be rewarded with a level of confidence, flow, focus, and collaboration that most creatives rarely experience.

AT A GLANCE:

THE VISION

Developing the core concept
to a detailed mental preview of the final work

A STRONG VISION PROVIDES BOTH THE ENGINE AND THE NAVIGATION SYSTEM FOR A SUCCESSFUL CREATIVE JOURNEY.

DRY STUDY

- GATHER INFORMATION
- CAPTURE OPTIONS

WET STUDY

- REHEARSE
- EXPERIMENT
- SOLVE PROBLEMS "OFF STAGE"

THE PREMAKE

FIRST YOU PREMAKE IT, THEN YOU MAKE IT.

- ANCHORS AND FOCUSES YOUR VISION
- ALLOWS YOU TO TEST YOUR VISION EARLY
- A GOOD PREMAKE IS: SIMPLE, BRIEF, CHEAP

THE SAFTEY RULES

- SET A TIME FRAME
- "MAYBE WE'LL USE IT"
- JUICE UP THE MUNDANE
- CHALLENGE YOUR PREMAKE

THE PRODUCTION

From Solid Vision to Refined Work

"Art is never finished, only abandoned."

Leonardo Da Vinci

Chapter **14**

The Artist
and the Critic

The Production stage is the longest and most demanding part of the creative workflow. With a diligently developed vision to support you, you'll be better prepared for it than most—but even so, it's easy to get overwhelmed and confused by the mass of details you need to take care of and by the new ideas that keep popping up as you work. This is also the part in which you find yourself inevitably "on stage," in front of your future audience—an open invitation for anxiety and fear of failure.

In this section, you'll learn an approach that's going to help you shake off the anxiety and confusion, and produce your final work with confidence and flow.

Dropped the Ball

To give you a clearer view of the challenges involved in the Production stage, here's a revealing little story of a minor Production disaster.

CAPTURE | CONCEPT | VISION | PRODUCTION | PLAN |

Many years ago, when I was making my first steps in the world of 3D animation, I thought I'd create my own little character to animate and experiment with. What I had in mind was simplicity itself: just a ball, with dots for eyes and sticks for arms and legs.

I fired up my 3D program and started building the character. I got so immersed in the work that I completely lost track of time for a good three hours or so. When I snapped out of it, I was *horrified* to find myself tweaking the muscles of the inner elbow of a very weird looking creature: half ball, half awkward-looking torso, with an almost realistic arm on one side and a shapeless stump on the other side (Figure 14.1).

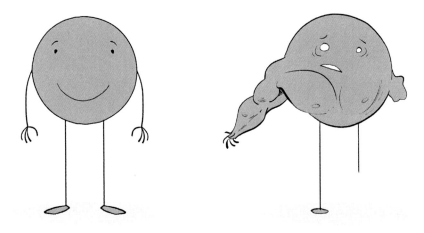

FIGURE 14.1 *A visualization of my original vision (left) vs. what I ended up with three hours later (right).*

Fixing the Fix

What happened there? How come I strayed so far from my original very simple idea?

When you're in the Production stage, you're playing two roles at the same time: you're both the *artist* doing the work and the *critic* judging it. Both these roles are important: they complement each other in the process of making a refined piece of creative work.

However, the fact that the same person (you) plays both roles creates a fundamental inner conflict. The experience is not unlike that of working with a demanding boss standing right over your shoulder, snapping at you every time you do something wrong. You know what that annoying boss sounds like: it's that voice inside your head that keeps saying things like, "This is wrong!" or "Why did I do this?" or "How could I have missed that?"

This, of course, is a toxic working environment for a creative. It means you're working in constant fear of making mistakes, and when a mistake does occur, you're compelled to immediately stop your work, zoom in, focus on that area, and fix it. As you do that, however, you inevitably make another small mistake. Your inner critic forces you to zoom in again and fix the smaller mistakes. But then, oops! You make another mistake. You zoom in again and fix that too…and before you know it, you find yourself tweaking the muscles of the inner elbow of something that was *supposed* to be a just ball with sticks for limbs (Figure 14.2).

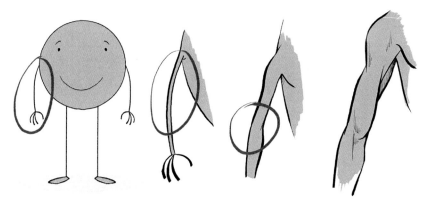

FIGURE 14.2   *The "zoom and fix" problem: every time you zoom in to fix a mistake, a smaller annoying mistake pops up.*

Consider this: that ball character was just a small and insignificant personal exercise—no deadlines, no high demands, no pay day, and only a few hours long. Now imagine something like that happening on a professional, large-scale, high-profile creative project—and I think you can see how horribly wrong things can go.

In fact, I'm willing to bet you don't really need to *imagine* it. We've all been there, and we all know how it feels.

Separation of Roles

Obviously, both roles are critical to success. We need the artist to create; we need the critic to point out problems. So, how do we resolve the conflict?

Once again, the solution is a healthy separation of the roles. Just like we've divided the entire creative process into three separate roles (the playful kid who dreams up the Concept, the curious teenager who develops the Vision, and the practical grownup who builds the artwork), we're now going to divide the Production process into two roles: *the artist* and *the critic*. We're going to tell your inner critic: "we value your opinion, but please *hold your judgment* for a short while and let the artist work in peace." Then, we're going to tell your inner artist: "go ahead and do a certain part of the work, then stop working and let the critic have a look" (Figure 14.3).

That "certain part of the work" your inner artist is going to work on is called a *pass*, and the process of moving back and forth between these two roles is called "working in passes."

FIGURE 14.3 *The artist and critic working at the same time (left) vs. separately (right).*

Here's how it works on a practical level:

Step 1: You create a rough capture of your vision.

Step 2: Your inner critic looks at the work and decides what needs to be improved for the next pass.

Step 3: Your inner artist steps in and works on the improvements suggested in step 2.

Step 4: If at the end of the pass you're out of time/budget/patience, or you feel the work is close enough to your vision, you're done. If not, you go back to step 2 and plan the next pass.

FIGURE 14.4 *Working in passes in a nutshell: you start with a very rough capture, then advance in simple steps toward your vision.*

This idea is so simple that it's hard to believe just how soothing and liberating it is. But don't confuse "simple" with "easy": working in passes takes time getting used to, and hides a few unpleasant pitfalls. In the next few chapters, we're going to take a look at the nuts and bolts of working in passes, and make sure you have a clear picture of how to get the most out of this process.

15

The First Pass

Just like with the Concept stage, the first step in Production is to make sure you're not starting with *nothing*. You want to have something to change.

Think of sculpting a bust in clay. Does it make sense to work on the base, then proceed to the neck, then the chin, and so on, all the way to the top? Of course not. Even if you're a complete newbie in clay, you'll intuitively begin with piling up a mass of clay in roughly the shape of your final bust. As rough and as wrong as it may be, at least now there's something for you to start shaping.

As it happens, this is the proper first step for *any* creative medium—even if it's not always as intuitive as it is in sculpting. Before you do anything else, you must create an initial crude version of the *entire piece*. It doesn't have to be good, it doesn't have to be correct, it doesn't have to be pretty. It just has to represent the entire thing. Never start with a first pass that captures only one chapter of your book, one screen of your mobile app, or one level of your game. You can focus on various parts later, but your first move *must* represent the entire scope of the work.

Let's take another example—something very unlike sculpting. What would your "something to change" pass look like if you were writing a book? Well, you'd pour out a few pages of text that roughly represent your idea of the final piece. It can be short, *spectacularly* wrong, and horribly written. All that doesn't matter. What matters is that you have a pile of text to work with that represents the full manuscript.

In fact, there's a good argument to be made that your first pass *needs* to be wrong—or, if not wrong, at least very crude. When you let your work grow organically from a simple seed, it often takes a life of its own and comes out unique and appealing. Starting too close to the ending point may cause the work to feel somewhat manufactured (Figure 15.1).

A   B

FIGURE 15.1 *Starting with an elaborated first pass may cause your work to feel cliched and manufactured (A). When you let your work grow organically from a simple seed, it often takes a life of its own and comes out unique and appealing (B).*

The Premake as the First Pass

Since the first "something to change" pass is a crude capture of the entire vision, you might argue that you already have such a capture: the premake, which you've created right before starting the Production process. Why not just use the premake as your first pass?

The answer is: you can often do that, but not always. That's because the purpose of the two captures is different. With the premake, the purpose is to lock and focus your vision. With the first pass, the purpose is to build the foundation out of which the final work will grow. A great premake will not always be a great first pass, and vice versa.

If you decide to use the premake as your first pass, make sure you're working with a copy and not the original premake itself. As we'll see in the next chapter, it's critical that your premake stays unchanged throughout the production process.

Chapter 16

The Critic

So, you've just completed a pass. Hopefully, your inner critic played ball and did not criticize your work while you were creating it; now, it's time to switch roles. Put down your tools and take a step back: you're no longer the artist. You are now the critic.

Asking the Right Question

As the critic, you're going to ask yourself a question, the answer to which will determine the next pass. You'll need to be very careful about the specific question you ask yourself, because it's going to define the quality of your Production process.

Many creatives simply ask themselves:

What's not working here?

This is an obvious and straightforward question; unfortunately, it is also the carrier of several creative maladies. The first and most important one is that it focuses your attention on the *negative* rather than the *positive*—thereby creating anxiety and self-doubt.

Let's try this question instead:

How can I improve this?

The difference may seem semantic, but it really isn't. The new question puts you in a positive and proactive mindset: not "I made a booboo and I need to fix it," but "this is great, here's how I can make it even better." What's more, the improvement question is more powerful: often, nothing is "broken" with the work, but it can still be greatly improved.

One thing the new question doesn't do is connect the improvement to the vision you have in mind. It's critical to make that connection, otherwise you may find yourself "improving" the work in an entirely wrong direction (we're going to talk more about the dangers of improving the work in the wrong way when we discuss *working in context*, in Chapter 23).

Here's an improved version:

What do I need to improve here, to get the work closer to my vision?

This is better. It's not only positive but also clearly directs your efforts toward the vision. One danger remains though: there is often *so* much to improve that the answer would be overwhelming. Let's try one last improvement:

What few and specific improvements would advance my work the farthest toward my vision?

This is a good question to ask yourself as you consider your work. It's positive, refers to your vision, and will generate simple and focused passes (which is the kind of passes we want). It also forces you to pay attention to priorities: major issues get worked out first, minor details, second.

Here's a comparison between the blunt "what's not working" question, and the more nuanced version. As you read through it, recall my Production disaster with the ball-and-sticks character: was it not the direct result of asking the wrong question?

What Few and Specific Improvements Would Advance My Work the Farthest Toward My Vision?	What's Not Working Here?
Positive (creates confidence)	Negative (creates self-doubt)
Refers to the vision	Takes a random direction
Generates short and focused passes	Possibly overwhelming
Important issues get resolved first	Random order

A Point of Reference

The question we've ended up with requires that you refer to the vision after each pass, compare it to the current state of the work, and determine the next pass accordingly. Luckily, you have a fixed point of reference to turn to—one that's easy to take in and that captures the most essential aspects of your vision. I'm talking about the premake, of course (Figure 16.1).

FIGURE 16.1 *Refer to the premake often (more than once a day) to make sure you're judging your work against a fixed, consistent vision. An easy-to-take-in premake will help you do that.*

You don't have to refer to the premake before each and every pass, especially if your passes are short and simple, but do make sure you take a glance at it several times during the day. Your inner critic may try to convince you that you don't need to look at the premake because you remember it well enough. Don't fall for it. The vision blurs and morphs in your head faster than you imagine. This is especially true in the more advanced passes, when you're dealing with minute details.

I mentioned in the previous section that a good premake can be taken in very quickly, almost at a glance. You can see now why that's important: if your premake can be taken in at a glance, you'll be able to refer to it often. If it takes too long or requires too much brainpower, it will either slow down the entire process or (more likely) be neglected completely.

By keeping your premake simple and referring to it often, you'll be able to avoid most of the confusion and anxiety that are so typical of the Production stage.

A Biased Judge

Being able to judge your work *objectively* against your vision can often make the difference between awesome and mediocre results. Unfortunately, objectivity is not an easy thing to achieve when you're critiquing your own work. Inevitably, you're going to be somewhat biased.

This isn't just a psychological thing. There's a physical side to it, too, and it has to do with the way the brain works. When you see something a certain way for a while, it gets engraved in your brain patterns in a way that makes it hard to see past it.

You can test it right now: take an image you know well—a picture you have on your wall, perhaps—and look at it through a mirror. If you've never tried it before, you're in for an interesting experience: you'll see this very familiar image in an entirely new way, probably even noticing some of the details for the first time. It will make you feel differently about it, too. That's because, even though it's the same image, your brain is suddenly experiencing it as something new. If you continue to look at it that way for a while, and then switch back to the original image, you'll get a similar sense of slight disorientation.

That means that, to improve your ability to judge your work, you should try to repeatedly change the way your brain perceives it. Yes, we're back to breaking hidden patterns; however, most of the pattern breakers we've discussed earlier don't make sense in the Production stage. Getting silly, changing your tools, or relying on external references don't really apply here.

Here are a few pattern breakers that *do* work.

Take a Break

This simple pattern breaker may cost time, but it works in every stage of the workflow, including the Production stage. Even a two-minute break between passes can make a difference. As always, do your best to take your mind off the work during the break: play a game, do a short workout, or have a conversation about something unrelated.

Change Your View

With this technique, we're trying to jolt your brain by forcing it to perceive the work in a new way—just like we did with the mirrored image. Different mediums offer different ways of doing that. Here are a few ideas:

- Change your physical position—take a few steps back or sideways. If you're using a computer software, change the scale or the orientation.

- Put it in a different environment—on a different background color, for example, or change the lighting (this last one is especially effective for sculpting).

CAPTURE | CONCEPT | VISION | PRODUCTION | PLAN

- If it's a piece of music, a video, or a game, try playing it faster or slower. Playing it backward could also be revealing.

- If your work is printable, print it! You'll see it in a whole new way. As an added bonus, you can now scribble notes and comments on the work itself.

- For visual artists, flipping the work every once in a while is a helpful habit to acquire. I use this all the time; in fact, in every program I use, I make sure I define a "flip" short-cut. I flip it, do a few passes, then flip it back again, and so on.

There are plenty of other tricks you can use: seeing it on a mobile screen instead of your monitor, projecting it on a wall, recording yourself and listening on different devices. Feel free to get creative and devise your own little tricks for seeing your work in a fresh way.

Put It in Its Context

In most types of projects, you'll be able to place your current pass in its context to judge it more clearly. Playing your animation shot in its sequence, pasting your architectural design on top of a picture of the street, placing the button design in its webpage context—these may not sound like pattern breakers, but they are. In fact, when it comes to changing the way you perceive your work, placing it in context is one of the strongest tools available to you.

I recently saw a demonstration in which a film segment was shown twice. The first time, it was shown as a regular video playing on a computer screen. The second time, it was played on the same computer screen, except this time, it was fitted into the context of a cinema environment, with an audience visible at the bottom of the screen (Figure 16.2). The effect was astonishing: because of the illusion of a bigger screen created by the context, the second screening felt completely different to me and changed my entire perception of the film's content.

FIGURE 16.2 *Putting your work in context can really change the way you (and other people) perceive it.*

Show It

Finally, showing your work to others is a pattern breaker that always works—no matter what stage of the process you're at. If you can show your pass to someone sharp and articulate who understands your vision, you might not need to be your own critic after all!

Critiquing with Both Sides of Your Brain

Whatever amount of objectivity you do manage is going to quickly wear off as you scrutinize your work. I'm talking about minutes; it's *that* fast (Figure 16.3).

FIGURE 16.3 *You lose most of your ability to judge the work objectivity within minutes, sometime even seconds. Make sure you listen hard to that precious first impression!*

Here's a technique I've developed as an animation director, which combines the benefits of quick judgment with the advantages of thorough scrutiny. It involves yet again the concept of right-brain thinking vs. left-brain thinking.

Step 1: Wet Scan

Experience your work once, very quickly, doing your best to see it as objectively as you can (you can use the pattern-breaking techniques described earlier). During that scan, focus on your *immediate emotional reactions*—but don't write anything yet. Just try to experience it as if you're part of your audience.

I call it the "wet scan" because, as with wet captures, you focus on the emotional/intuitive part of your brain and consider the piece as a whole rather than as an assortment of different parts.

Step 2: Capture

When you're done, capture your impressions as fast as you can. If you need another quick scan to make sure you got it all down, that's fine.

Step 3: The Dry Scan

Now, go through the piece again, and this time, slow down. Look into the details and technical aspects of the work, and try to figure out what made you react the way you did in the wet scan. Keep the list short, but don't limit yourself too much. Capture your thoughts as they come.

I call it the "dry scan" because it's a more analytical kind of scrutiny that focuses on the parts rather than the whole and therefore relies on the left side of your brain.

Make sure you do your wet scan first and dry scan later, and that you treat your dry scan as an analysis of the wet scan—not as a separate thing. It'll help you design a simple and coherent pass that has a certain theme to it. This will save you from being overwhelmed by details.

A Shopping List

The final product of the critic's job is a "shopping list" of improvements you'd like your inner artist to take care of in the next pass. This could be an actual written list, but it can also take other forms: a bunch of Post-it notes, scribbles, marks you make directly on the work itself, or any combination of the above (Figure 16.4).

Make sure your shopping list of improvements is not too long. Don't dump an overwhelming and arbitrary pile of changes on your poor inner artist; instead, try to design passes that have a clear title, or at least a sense of inner logic: "dialogue pass," "textures pass," "facial anatomy pass," etc. Pick the few most important improvements that fall under that title and leave the rest for future passes. The wet/dry critiquing method explained above will also help you do that.

In addition, try to stay away from vague or negative notes ("this color looks weird"). Such a note is going to send your inner artist in a random direction and could create confusion and anxiety. Instead, make sure your inner artist receives well-defined notes ("Let's try a warmer color"). Such a note leaves room for

CAPTURE | CONCEPT | VISION | PRODUCTION | PLAN

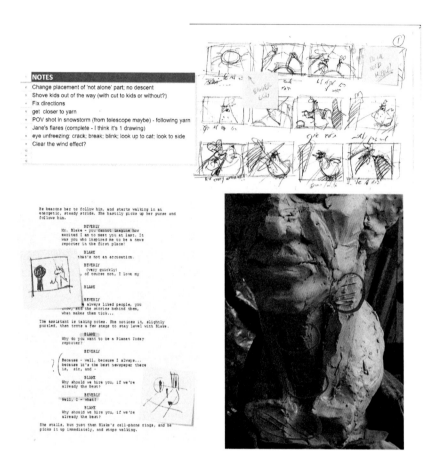

FIGURE 16.4 *Shopping list. Your "shopping list" can be an actual list—or it can be Post-it notes, scribbles, or marking the work itself.*

improvisation and creativity while providing a positive direction and a healthy framework for your inner artist to work within.

In the next chapter, we'll talk more about the benefits of keeping to that framework.

Chapter 17

The Artist

Let's talk about something creatives don't usually enjoy talking about: discipline.

As creatives, we love diving into our work, losing ourselves in it while we tinker with the juicy details. When it's done in a disciplined way, that's great; when it's unmanaged, it can be disastrous—as we've seen in the beginning of this section.

The trick is to let your inner artist dive in and have fun with the work, but only within the well-defined boundaries of the pass. These are the boundaries I'm referring to:

The boundaries of the critic's list. The critic's list of improvements defines the current pass. As the artist, you should keep to it: fixing or improving things that aren't on the list goes against the whole concept of this workflow. Within the list, you can get as creative as you like, but keep everything that's not on the list for future passes. Also, make sure you *stop working* when you've completed the pass. It's tempting to just keep at it, especially when you feel things are flowing well; but working in passes is about building mutual respect between your inner artist and your inner critic, and it's not your inner artist's job to determine the next set of improvements. Once the list is done, stop working, change hats, and let the critic direct your efforts.

The boundaries of time. Before you begin, you'll need to decide on a time frame for the pass. An open-ended pass is an invitation for problems. Most passes should take somewhere between 10 minutes and an hour, although some passes can be a lot shorter than that. Aim for doing the entire pass without a break, and try not to go past two hours for a single pass.

The boundary of direction. Your pass should have a clear and constant forward thrust. Barring small course corrections, you should get used to *not* going back and editing your work during the pass. Remember that your inner artist has a limited ability to judge the result; I can't tell you how many times I've worked hard on something that looked a certain way from my artist's perspective, only to have to undo the work when looking at it with the critic's eye. Keep going forward and rely on the critic to suggest changes later on.

A Fenced Playground

The idea of working with "discipline" and "boundaries" may sound unpleasantly restrictive, when in fact it is liberating.

Consider the following experiment: two teachers take two groups of kids to play at two local playgrounds. One playground is fenced, the other is not. In which scenario would the children feel more free? As it turns out, the children in the unfenced playground tend to stay close to the teacher and the playground equipment, while the children in the fenced playground tend to spread out and use the entire fenced space.

Here's a similar example that many of us would recognize from everyday life. Think of parking your car in an open and unmarked area: if there's a car already parked there, most people will park right next to it. In a well-defined parking lot, they would usually park further away.

The point is that defined boundaries create clarity, which creates confidence, which creates a sense of freedom. In the context of working in passes, when you have a well-defined pass and you're disciplined enough to keep to its boundaries, you get to work with greater confidence. Within those boundaries, you can allow yourself to try things, make mistakes, and be playful without the fear of spoiling your work or getting hopelessly entangled in the details.

Detecting Trouble

With a simple and well-defined pass, your inner artist's workflow will usually be fairly smooth. Usually, but not *always*: creativity is a fundamentally unpredictable business, and sometimes things just get messy. That's not a problem in and of it self—as long as you notice it early enough and do something about it.

This is easier said than done: most of us get caught up in the inertia of our work, not realizing we're sinking in creative quicksand until we're already neck deep.

Here are a few warning signs to help you detect trouble early.

Exceeding the timeframe. If you've set a time frame of 45 minutes for the pass, and you're now well past the two-hour mark, that's a clear sign something's wrong. This is your only objective and quantifiable sign of trouble—don't ignore it!

Mounting anxiety and/or confusion. When everything is as it should be, a pass should flow almost naturally and be fun to do. Once a pass becomes irritating or frustrating, or if you feel increasingly confused about what you're doing, you should take it as a sign that something's wrong.

Shifting between minor details and sweeping changes. This will be further explained in the next chapter, but basically, passes that combine big structural changes with tweaking of minor details are a sign of trouble. The same goes for big swings in the level of changes between consecutive passes.

Unclear boundaries. If you find yourself working on a pass that has no clear list of improvements to take care of, a clear time-frame, or a clear aim, that means you're not really working in passes anymore. Whatever creative process you're practicing, it's not the one described in this book.

Course Correction

What should you do upon realizing your pass has gone off course?

Well, the first thing to do is to *stop working*. You won't get yourself unstuck by stepping harder on the gas: you need to figure out what's causing the problem first. Take a small break to clear your mind and break thinking patterns, then come back and focus on solving the *process* rather than the work itself.

First, make sure your work still follows your vision/premake. Sometimes, when we don't pay enough attention to the premake over a few passes, the work drifts away and detaches itself from the vision. If that's the case, all you need to do is go back and realign your vision, your premake, and your work. If you've been alert to the signs of trouble and detected it early enough, this shouldn't be a big deal at all; and, at least you know what went wrong and how to fix it!

If the work is aligned to your vision but you still feel confused, try the following remedies:

Design a new pass. Stop the pass, put on your critic cap again, and come up with a new list of improvements. Sometimes, the very act of redefining the boundaries will solve the problem. You might also want to make the new pass simpler and shorter; the original one may have been too ambitious.

Go back to a previous pass. If you've crawled too far down the rabbit hole of confusion, crawling back might be the solution. If you're working in a digital medium, you might be able to go back to a saved previous pass. I usually save a version of my work after every pass I've completed so that I can easily "rewind" my work to a version in which I still knew what I was doing.

A reset pass. When rewinding isn't possible, I often undo the chaos by dry capturing my existing work. Because each pass is basically a capture of a more advanced pass, this is really another form of rewinding. Doing a dry capture will eliminate confusing details and redefine the structure, which should help you regain control.

Enjoy the View

The artist has a simple, straightforward role. Using the hiking metaphor from the previous section, your inner artist's job is just to walk along the trail already charted and enjoy the view. For the length of a pass, you get to give your brain a rest: don't think too much, don't make big decisions, and don't get too inventive. Allow yourself to be simple for this role. Keep to the trail, and just let things flow naturally and effortlessly. To me, that's a big part of what makes this entire workflow so enjoyable.

Chapter 18

Advanced Production Topics

We've discussed the critic, the artist, and the workflow of shifting between those two roles. At this point, however, you may be feeling that the process I've described is not very practical: an interesting theory, perhaps, but too slow and cumbersome for real life.

I can readily agree that it *feels* that way. This is partly because explaining it is a lot more cumbersome than doing it, but also, the idea of starting with a rough approximation and improving it in small and simple steps does *feel* intuitively slow.

To see why that feeling is deceptive, let's take a step back and look at the overall shape of the process.

Straight Stairs Going Up

In explaining the next few points, I'm going to use the term *zoom level* quite a lot. By that I just mean the level of details you're focused on at a given moment. The broader your view is, the more "zoomed out" you are; the smaller the details you're tweaking, the more "zoomed in" you are.

Generally speaking (there are always exception to the rule when it comes to creativity!), a healthy pass should be kept at a relatively consistent zoom level, so that by the end of the pass, the entire work is more or less evenly refined. The reason this is important is that ending a pass with an uneven level of refinement makes it hard for your inner critic to figure out what needs to be improved. Figure 18.1 shows a simplified visualization of that challenge.

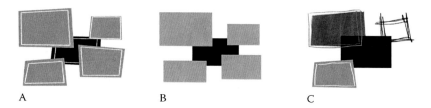

A B C

FIGURE 18.1 *(A) The vision we're trying to get to; (B) example of an **even pass**; (C) example of an **uneven pass**.*

Drawing (A) represents your vision. Drawing (B) represents an *even pass*. As you can see, even though it is quite basic, it's clear what stage the work is at. That's because everything is on the same level of refinement. Possible improvements present themselves readily: add a white line, change the positions and scales of the elements to match the vision, distort rectangles to make them funkier, etc.

Drawing (C) represents an *uneven pass*, with different parts at different levels of refinement. Notice how difficult it gets to define a clear next pass. Thus, although obviously more labored than drawing (B), it is actually in worse shape.

So a healthy pass starts at an even state, keeps to a consentient zoom level, and ends with the entire work being at a more refined even state. This leads us to the next point: in a healthy Production workflow, as the work progresses, you should see a gradual increase in the zoom level of individual passes. If the zoom level stays constant over too many passes, or if it seems to move erratically up and down, that indicates a problem.

Let's put it all together and see what we've got so far. Looking at the shape of your process on a timeline (Figure 18.2), you should expect a reasonably clean shape of "straight stairs going up."

Each stair is a pass (or a group of passes), and the idea is to keep the "stairs" straight and equal.

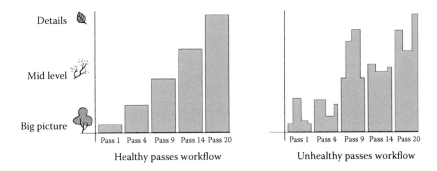

Healthy passes workflow   Unhealthy passes workflow

FIGURE 18.2   *The shape of a healthy passes workflow vs. an unhealthy one. In a healthy workflow, the* **zoom level** *is kept generally constant throughout each individual pass and steadily increases through the progression of passes. Notice how, in the unhealthy workflow, the zoom level is irregular both within and between the passes. If this is the shape of your workflow, stop working and figure out why.*

Explosive Progress

This is where we get to the confusing bit—the reason this process feels slow, even though it isn't. Here's the nub: although the *increase in zoom level* between passes stays more or less constant throughout the work, the *progress* you make is not constant at all.

To understand why, try to imagine the gap between your first pass and your vision as a long strip of paper. With each pass, you're cutting the strip in half; in other words, you're removing half of the "wrongness" in your work (that's a gross oversimplification, but correct in principle). At first, you'll chop away big pieces of paper, but after just a few quick steps, you're going to find yourself needing a magnifying glass. So, each pass is equally simple and chips away the same *rate* of "wrongness," but the *amount* of "wrongness" gets smaller and smaller as the work gets closer to the vision.

Figure 18.3 shows a visualization of that principle, where the vision is represented by a perfect circle, and the first pass is represented by a shapeless "amoeba". The digital sculpture process shows the exact same effect.

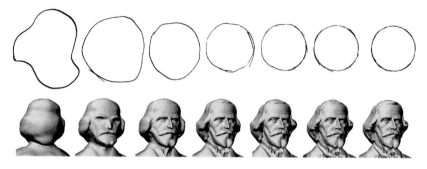

FIGURE 18.3 *Each pass is equally simple and chips away the same **rate** of "wrongness," but the **amount** of "wrongness" gets smaller and smaller as the work gets closer to the vision.*

The takeaway is that, when you work in simple and steady passes, the result is not the tediously slow and steady progress you might expect. Instead, the progress is *explosive*: fast and furious in the first few passes, then slowing down considerably as you increase the zoom level and focus on the details (Figure 18.4).

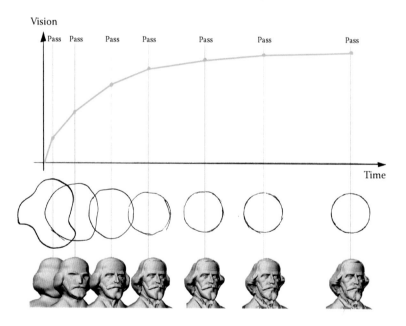

FIGURE 18.4 *Explosive progress. As you increase the zoom level and focus on smaller and smaller details, the pace of improvement slows down considerably—both in the amount of time each pass requires and the breadth of change it creates.*

The Bottom Line

What should you make of all this?

To start with, explosive progress allows you to collaborate better. The steep progress curve at the beginning of the process means you get to show your work in a state that's *advanced* enough for others to make sense of and give feedback on, and yet is *early* enough in the process to allow you to put that feedback into effect. This is something your clients, supervisors, and team members are going to appreciate a lot.

Another takeaway is that working in passes provides you with a kind of "safety area." Here's what I mean: suppose you have a project in which you're budgeted for 10 passes. However, something goes wrong and you end up only having time/budget for seven passes. If you're not working in passes, losing 30% of your resources* probably means you're in trouble. With explosive progress on your side, you're actually in great shape: for the layman, the quality difference is going to be almost unnoticeable.

Finally—and perhaps most importantly—the explosive progress graph shows you the realistic cost of quality. You can get to "okay" quite quickly, but "excellent" takes a long time: going up just 10% in quality could easily take twice the amount of time! This is an important thing to keep in mind because it's not very intuitive: the human brain tends to think linearly, not exponentially. Being aware of this principle is going to help you plan (and price) you work more realistically and avoid a lot of unnecessary stress.

We're going to talk more about project planning in the next section. For now, let's wrap things up with a couple of safety rules.

---

* More than 30%, in fact. Look at the explosive progress graph again: since the last passes are typically much longer than the the the first ones, doing only 7 passes out of 10 probably means you've cut the project by more half.

Chapter 19

The Production
Safety Rules

Let Your Mind Lead the Way

In studying the creative workflow, one of the most important and beneficial principles I've discovered was the principle of *leading with your mind*.

What do I mean by that?

As you work on each pass, you should always try to see in your mind's eye the work as it will be a few passes in the future, so that your current pass is really a *capture* of a more advanced pass. As you develop your work, this "short-term vision," if you will, gradually becomes more and more detailed (see Figure 19.1). Think of it as a chase, in which your work tries to catch up with your vision but the vision keeps being two or three steps ahead. The goal is to keep the chase going until the very end; once your work catches up with your vision, it's "game over."

Here's a good visual metaphor to keep in mind: imagine driving in the middle of the night on an unfamiliar and dark road. What you're focusing on is *not* what's happening right now under your

CAPTURE | CONCEPT | VISION | PRODUCTION | PLAN

FIGURE 19.1 *In this illustration, (A) is the current pass and (B) is the pass I see in my mind's eye—not fully detailed, not completely clear, but enough to know where I'm heading. Panel (C) is a visual representation of how that process feels: I draw (A) while having (B) in mind. Panel (D) is the final illustration, made for a children's book.*

car. Instead, at any given moment, you're looking at what's happening at the far end of your headlights. You want your actions right *now* to be influenced by *that* information. Even if you *could* drive fast enough to catch up with your lights, you wouldn't want to, because you'd crash. In the same way, even if you *can* catch up with your vision in any given pass, you shouldn't. Keep that healthy gap, and only let it close on your very last pass.

The safety rule: don't let your work catch up to your vision! Let your mind lead the way.

FIGURE 19.2 *Your work chases the vision, trying to close the gap; don't let it catch up!*

Stick to Your Vision

Often, a new and shiny idea will suddenly pop up during the production stage and take you by storm. It's going to make your current vision seem like the most mundane and unexciting piece of yesterday's news. The temptation to change course is going to be immense.

It is, of course, the song of the siren. If you've done your Concept stage properly, chances are the new idea isn't really better—it's just *different*. It probably has to do with one of the following two [false] reasons:

New is exciting. You've gotten used to your current vision, and it's not as new and exciting to you anymore. In this case, pretty much *any* change would feel like it's better than the original vision.

New is easy. There's a practical difficulty with the vision: a hard problem to solve or maybe a boring section you need to plow through. In this case, your brain will sometimes try to convince you that some other vision that seems easier to achieve is actually also better; why waste time on this difficult thing, when there's a wonderful alternative that looks much easier to do?

If you fall for it—if you change direction mid-course—you'll almost certainly sentence yourself to failure and frustration down the road. It's not just the fact you've already invested some time in the current idea and that changing now will force you to start patching things up. The real and more severe problem is that as soon as you turn your back on your premake (and the vision it represents), you no longer have a clear goal with a fixed point of reference. That means you've stepped out of the controlled workflow and have exposed yourself to all the usual dangers and pitfalls of creativity: confusion, overwhelm, fear of failure, and a general lack of structure and control.

In my studies of the creative process, I've seen countless examples of projects that started with a great premake and were moving along nicely until at some point, the creator suddenly decided to change course. In these cases, almost without exception, the final work was inferior to the promise of the premake.

That said, as I've been saying repeatedly, creativity is an inherently chaotic and unpredictable business. Sometimes, you do have to move away from your initial vision. This could be a change in the client's needs, a significant shift in your own point of view, or perhaps the vision really doesn't work as expected. What then?

The answer is: first, make sure this isn't a whim. Break your patterns to see the situation more objectively, consult other people, and generally make an effort to fight for your original vision (after all, you did believe in it at one point). If you're still confident that it needs to change, the only safe way to do it is to do the vision stage all over again: study your new concept, develop a new Vision, create a new premake, and then start your Production process from scratch.

The safety rule: never change your concept mid-production. Stick to your vision, and if you can't, go back and create a new one.

CAPTURE — CONCEPT — VISION

PRODUCTION

PLAN

Conclusion

This concludes our discussion of the Production stage.

We've analyzed the schizophrenic challenge of being both the artist and the critic, and introduced the *working in passes* workflow as a way of alleviating that problem. We then discussed this workflow in some length, but the principle remains very simple indeed: after completing each pass, you *stop working*, evaluate your work, decide how to proceed, and then work according to that plan. That's all there is to it; the rest is just fine-tuning.

That said, working in passes is one of those things that are simple to learn but hard to master. It requires you to keep a certain part of your mind acutely aware of the process, even as you create your work. That's a difficult thing to do when you're "on stage" trying to give as much attention as possible to your craft. Perhaps even more challenging is the discipline part of it: keeping to the boundaries of the pass, resisting the urge to fix obvious mistakes, and keeping the passes simple—even though so much is left to work on and the deadline is looming.

For all those reasons, being able to have a smooth Production stage on a demanding project is going to take some time and practice. All I can do is assure you that it's going to be worth your while. Once *gradual improvement* becomes second nature to you and replaces the focus on *immediate perfection*, you'll be able to realize any creative vision at the highest level of control, confidence and refinement.

AT A GLANCE:

THE PRODUCTION

From "something to change"
to a refined piece

**DON'T FIX IT - JUST IMPROVE IT,
ONE SIMPLE STEP AT A TIME**

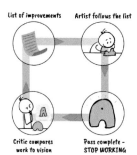

WORKING IN PASSES

List of improvements   Artist follows the list

Critic compares   Pass complete -
work to vision   STOP WORKING

THE CRITIC'S QUESTION

~~"WHAT'S WRONG HERE?"~~

*"WHICH FEW AND SPECIFIC
IMPROVEMENTS WOULD ADVANCE MY
WORK THE FURTHEST TOWARD MY
VISION?"*

ADVANCED CONCEPTS

- EVEN PASSES
-" STRAIGHT STEPS GOING UP"
- EXPLOSIVE PROGRESS

 ## THE SAFTEY RULES

- LET YOUR MIND LEAD THE WAY
- STICK TO YOUR VISION

THE PLAN

Managing Your Workflow

"The secret of getting ahead is getting started. The secret of getting started is breaking your complex overwhelming tasks into small manageable tasks, and starting on the first one."

Mark Twain

Chapter 20

The Manager

When I gave you the overview of the workflow, back in Section I, I mentioned that each of the three main stages—Concept, Vision, and Production—requires a different mindset. It's like you're moving between three distinct creative personas—a virtual inner dream team of experts. Each expert has a specific job to do and knows exactly how to do it; but just like any other team, in order to work effectively together, they need a good *manager*. Without proper management, even the simplest project may fall into disarray.

The Simplest of Plans

Here's one cautionary tale out of many.

A couple of years back, I was sharing a workspace with a designer. Her inner Concept, Vision, and Production personas were very capable, but because most of her gigs were short and simple, her inner manager persona was practically nonexistent.

Eager to try more challenging projects, she was thrilled when she finally landed a particularly juicy one. It was longer and more demanding than her usual gigs, but she had enough time to do it right; in fact, she was given more time than she actually needed. Sounds perfect, doesn't it?

Here's what happened.

Since she had so much time on her hands, her inner team of personas did what most teams do when the manager is out and the deadline is far away: they procrastinated. It took her a few days to even start working on it, and when she did, she spent an entire day on a small and rather insignificant element of the work. This wasn't intentional at all—she just got sucked into it and lost track of time. Because she had all that extra time on her hands, she didn't mind so much. The next morning, however, she realized she was so focused on that one little element that she took it way too far and would have to completely redo it.

Shortly after that unpleasant realization, her clients called. They wanted to know when they could see something.

Since at that point she was supposed to have been working on the project for about a week, she didn't want to admit she had nothing to show yet. So, she promised to show them something the next morning and started working frantically to make that happen. Unfortunately, that put her in so much stress that it made things worse: she was thrown into a spiral of confusion and anxiety, and the next morning, she *still* had nothing worthwhile to show. At this point, she was coming very close to losing both the project and the client. The fun and laidback project became a complete nightmare.

Working in the same room with her, I could see something was very wrong. When she told me the story, my first question was: "what's your plan?"

She gave me a blank stare. "What do you mean? I'm just...working on it."

When everything goes crazy, it's critical to stop what you're doing, take a step back, assess the situation as objectively as possible, and make a plan. When I suggested that to her, she freaked out. "I have no time for planning—I need to work!"

I told her she didn't have time *not* to plan.

To help her break the anxiety cycle, we left the studio and went to a nearby coffee shop. After 15 minutes, we had a list of six tasks, each attached to a specific timeframe: 40 minutes for this, 60 minutes for that, and so on (Figure 20.1). We agreed that whatever happens, she will not spend a second longer on any given task— even if it turns out bad. When time's up, she would stop and proceed to the next task.

This completely transformed the situation for her. Before the list, everything she did felt like it was taking too long, and that stressed her out and made it difficult to focus. Now that she had the list, she felt on more solid ground. The pressure was still there, but it was now working *for* her rather than *against* her. When you're not in control of a situation, pressure creates anxiety and makes you less effective; but when you're in control, pressure creates hyperfocus and makes you *more* effective.

In the end, this simplest of plans was enough to stop her spinning, give her a sense of control, and ultimately save the project.

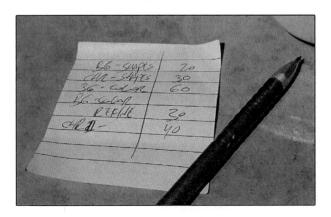

FIGURE 20.1   *This simple schedule, scribbled on a piece of paper in a coffee shop, was enough to take the sting out of a very nasty situation.*

CAPTURE | CONCEPT | VISION | PRODUCTION | PLAN

Amplifying Creativity

Some creatives bear a level of resentment to the idea of managing their work. They feel like real-world issues like deadlines and efficiency somehow stand in the way of creativity and "defile" the purity of art. In this section, I hope to convince you that, far from inhibiting your creativity, good management will actually protect and even inspire it.

Coming up next is a set of advanced planning techniques that support and amplify the workflow methods we've discussed so far.

Chapter **21**

Linear Chunking

All planning starts with *linear chunking*. That simply means dividing your work to logical sections and allocating a certain amount of time for each task. As we've seen, even a simple list can be tremendously helpful.

In this chapter, we'll take it a couple of steps further.

The Seven Standard Chunks

The three main stages of the creative workflow discussed in this book—Concept, Vision, and Production—provide us with a great starting point for chunking a project. Let's add a timeframe to each chunk.

A good rule of the thumb for small- and medium-sized projects is to allocate 25%–40% of the time to Concept and Vision, leaving 60%–75% for the Production stage (Figure 21.1). The Concept state is usually quite short, which means most of the pre-production time would be dedicated to developing your Vision.

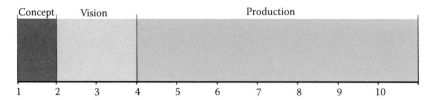

FIGURE 21.1 *Three chunks. Let's say you have 10 days to complete a proj-ect. A typical basic plan would be as follows:* **one day** *to come up with a strong concept,* **two days** *to develop a vision and create the premake, and seven days to create the finished work.*

Now, let's gain more control by adding a second level of chunking (chunk the chunks, if you will). The Concept stage is short enough that we don't need to chunk it further, so let's start with the Vision stage. Here, too, we have a natural division: the dry study, the wet study, and the premake (Figure 21.2).

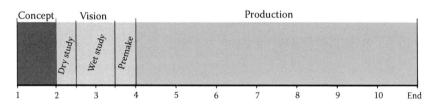

FIGURE 21.2 *Dividing the vision stage.*

We're now getting to the Production stage, and here we have a problem: although Production is naturally chunked to *passes*, it's impossible to plan those in advance. Each pass is planned by the critic in response to the current state of the work. How many passes will you need? How long will they take? There's no way of knowing.

If we're going to have a plan, we'll need to find a different chunk-ing approach.

The method I found to be useful in most situations is to chunk the Production stage into three sections: *blocking*, *shaping*, and *refining*.

If you imagine your work as a human body, the blocking section would be like building the skeleton: a solid framework of struc-ture that holds the work together. Shaping is where you "put flesh on the bones," giving your work a clear shape. Finally, the refining section is where you add the details and texture that make your work beautiful and complete. In our human body metaphor, this would be akin to adding the skin, hair, eyelashes, etc. (Figure 21.3).

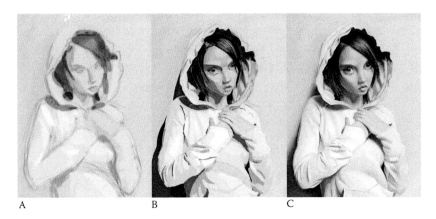

A   B   C

FIGURE 21.3   Blocking, shaping, and refining in painting: (A) blocking with big shapes, (B) shaping—giving it a more defined shape, (C) refining—adding details and texture. (Art courtesy of Rafi Ben Aharon.)

How much time should you schedule for each section? The answer depends on many factors: the kind of project you're working on, the scope of it, the level of refinement you're going for, your own personal creative style, and so on. You'll have to experiment a bit to discover what works for you. The important bit is, that you now have three distinct sections that you can chunk the Production stage into, without having to know how many passes each section would contain.

Looking at the entire process, you now have seven standard chunks that you can use for planning and managing your creative projects (Figure 21.4).

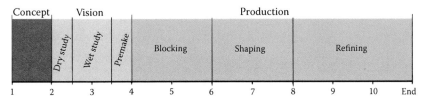

FIGURE 21.4   Seven chunks. An example of a project scheduled according to the seven standard chunks. Remember that, depending on various factors, the specific time frames allocated to each chunk may change.

This is perhaps a good place to mention that not every project requires all three stages of the creative process. Sometimes, you won't need the Concept part because you'll have a specific task for which the concept is a given. Other times, you won't need to do much studying—perhaps because you're already very familiar with the techniques and materials involved. Even the Production stage is not always required: sometimes, the main part of the project is to come up with the vision. Pay attention to what the project demands, and make sure you schedule your work accordingly.

Micro-Deadlines

On short projects—a few days long at the most—the seven standard chunks provide a reasonable level of control. On longer projects, you'll want to have more than seven chunks, so that each chunk isn't too long. In the 10-day-long project we've been using as an example, the blocking chunk is planned to take two whole days—and that's much too long for one continuous stretch of work. In fact, the ideal time frame for a chunk is less than two hours. That's roughly the amount of time the average creative can stay super-focused, without taking a break.

The graph in Figure 21.5 explains why short chunks are more effective.

As you can see, the more effective approach is to work in short, hyperfocused bursts, taking plenty of breaks in between. I call these smaller chunks *micro-deadlines*: little challenges you give yourself throughout the day. Everything we've been talking about so far supports the idea of micro-deadlines and is supported by it: in both the Concept stage and the Vision stage, I've pointed out the need to define specific timeframes for different tasks. As for the Production stage, micro-deadlines fit the bill perfectly: we've been discussing the merits of setting a timeframe for each pass and of keeping the passes short and focused.

Working with micro-deadlines may sound too strict or tedious, but once you get used to the idea, they can actually be fun. They turn your day from a long and often monotonous experience to

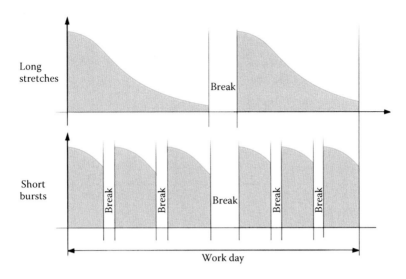

FIGURE 21.5   *Working in long continuous stretches (top) vs. short "hyperfocused" bursts (bottom). The painted areas show the amount of actual progress being made. Notice the improved productivity, despite spending more time in breaks.*

something of a game: you set yourself these little challenges and try to make them happen. Can I do this in 15 minutes? Can I do that in an hour? And, just like with a game, you get the added satisfaction of seeing yourself getting better at it.

Adaptive Planning

The problem with planning micro-deadlines is the same problem we had with passes: you can't plan them in advance because you don't know what they're going to be. Even if you did, planning at that level of detail is simply impractical.

If *macro-planning* (the seven chunks) is too loose and *micro-planning* is too rigid, how do you plan your project?

The solution is to combine the two in an adaptive plan that you keep updating as you proceed. To demonstrate, let's return to our hypothetical 10-day project.

Imagine you're at the beginning of day 4: you have your Concept and Vision ready, and you're now going to start the blocking part of your Production process. Before you begin, you put your planning cap on and, to the best of your ability, chunk up the few upcoming days to clear tasks. Perhaps you end up with something like that shown in Figure 21.6.

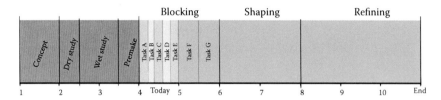

FIGURE 21.6   *In this example, we chunk day 4 (current day) to micro-deadlines, and day 5 is chunked to just two half-days. Days 6 to 10 remain as macro-chunks for now.*

Let's imagine that at the end of day 4, things are going more or less according to plan—but not entirely: you ended up doing only four out of the five micro-chunks (you need another hour or so for the remaining chunk). At the beginning of day 5, you'll again spend a few minutes planning and chunking ahead, taking into account the realities of the previous day. The new plan may look like this:

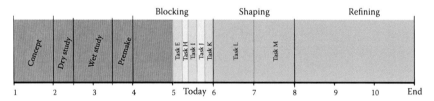

FIGURE 21.7   *Day 5. The new plan: day 5 is now chunked to micro-deadlines (these include the remaining chunk from the previous day). Looking further ahead, you may already chunk the shaping stage to two tasks, one for each day.*

With this approach, upcoming tasks get scheduled more tightly, while the planning of more distant tasks stays loose and easy to change. Thus, you get to enjoy both worlds: the hyperfocus and control of micro-deadlines, with the flexibility and clear structure of macro chunking.

Active and Responsive

Clearly, the adaptive planning approach requires constant attention and managing. That's a good thing: active management means you're keeping yourself attentive to your project's needs and responding to changes as they happen. That's the key to a creative workflow in which all the different elements work together optimally. It also means you'll be spending 10–15 minutes every morning (or evening) updating your plan; however, I hope I've been able to convince you that the effectivity and sense of control it creates justify that investment.

Make sure you have your plan written down; it should not be inside your head. Some people use a piece of paper; others use sophisticated scheduling software. Both work; it's a matter of personal preference. Personally, I like using a simple spreadsheet: it's easier to update than a piece of paper and does not force you to use someone else's management paradigms. You can try it out with my template spreadsheet, available on the book's website.

The Next Step

In this chapter, we've discussed *linear planning*. It's linear in the sense that whichever way you chunk your project, the schedule is always essentially a string of tasks arranged on a single timeline and carried out one by one. This is an excellent approach for simple projects, but for more complex projects, it has several serious drawbacks. In the next chapter, we'll look into a much more powerful chunking approach with which you'll be able to manage projects of any size or level of complexity.

Chapter 22
Scaling Up

As you may have noticed, the workflow I've described so far would only work well for projects done by a single person over a few weeks at the most. Writing an article, designing a simple website, animating a shot or a short sequence—these are the kinds of projects that work well with linear chunking.

When things get bigger and more complex, the linear Concept–Vision–Production workflow starts breaking at the seams. Imagine the project from the previous chapter taking not 10 *days* to complete, but 10 *months*. In that case, each of the seven standard chunks we've been talking about is going to take several weeks. That's such a long timeframe that adaptive planning and two-hour-long micro-deadlines just don't cut it anymore (pun intended). It's simply too overwhelming.

There are also issues beyond time management. Take the idea of working in passes, for example: the whole Production workflow is based on your inner critic reviewing the work between passes. That's fine if you're writing an article, but what if you're working

CAPTURE | CONCEPT | VISION | PRODUCTION | PLAN

on a 300-page-long novel? Obviously, you can't read the entire thing before every two-hour pass.

Then there's the issue of teamwork. Most large-scale projects aren't done by a single person. How do you work the scheme of Concept–Vision–Production with several creatives working in parallel? How do you work in passes in that situation?

For projects in that scale, we'll have to change our approach. In this chapter, we're going to abandon the linear way of thinking and start thinking in *fractals*.

Breaking the Broccoli

Fractals are super-complex structures created with a few simple rules. Those rules repeat themselves over and over again, in different scales, so that no matter how closely you look at the fractal, you'll always see the same kind of pattern. Once you know what you're looking for, you'll find them everywhere: from galaxies to mountains to snowflakes, nature is full of fractals. In fact, you can find one of the most striking examples of fractal structures in your local supermarket. It's called Romanesco broccoli (see Figure 22.1).

FIGURE 22.1 *Romanesco broccoli is a striking example of fractal structure: every piece of it, no matter what size, looks like the entire broccoli.*

How does that relate to the creative workflow?

Well, as I've already hinted in several places in this book, sometimes, sections of a large creative project can be treated as full-fledged creative projects in and of themselves.

For example, an animated feature film goes through the standard workflow of Concept, Vision + premake, and finally, the full Production. Let's focus on the premake for the film, called an *animatic*. It's a crude representation of the director's vision of the film, made with a few thousand drawings and edited with temp music and voice acting. Creating the animatic typically takes more than a year, with around 15 artists and editors working full-time. This is quite a large creative project by any standard, and at the same time, it's just the premake for an even larger project.

In fact, the animatic is such a big project that it needs to be chunked to still smaller subprojects, called *sequences*. Drawing a sequence typically takes a single storyboard artist about two or three weeks. Now, we're finally back to our linear Concept–Vision–Production workflow, and we already know how to manage that. This relatively tiny subproject—a small piece of the films' premake—is going to need its own premake, of course.

As you can see, a large-scale creative project works exactly like a fractal structure: the scale changes, but the rules of the workflow stay the same.

Here's what it means on a practical level: when you have a large or complex project on your hands, instead of breaking it up to simple tasks, you'll want to break it to smaller *subprojects*. You don't cut it like a cucumber; that's linear thinking. Instead, you break it apart like Romanesco broccoli. Then you can work on each "branch" of the broccoli separately, using the exact same methods you've used for the bigger project. And if the smaller subproject is still too complex, no problem—you can break it down again, and then again, until you get to a chunk that's simple enough to be managed with the linear workflow (Figure 22.2).

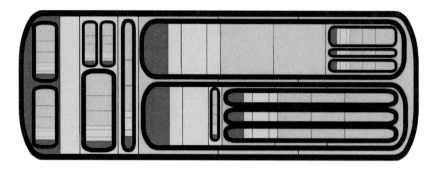

FIGURE 22.2 *Fractal chunking: break your large or complex project down to smaller subprojects, then work on each "branch" of the broccoli separately, using the exact same methods you've used for the bigger project.*

Layers and Slices

Let me switch metaphors here, just for this one section. I'd like you to imagine your creative project not as a broccoli but as a rich layer cake.

There are two ways of dividing that cake. You can divide it into *layers*—the base, the cream, the chocolate, the fruit, etc.; or you can divide it to *slices* (Figure 22.3).

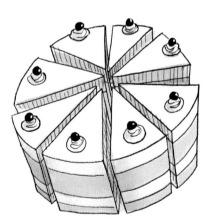

FIGURE 22.3 *Layers vs. slices.*

Chunk your project into layers when it involves *different types of tasks*, to be completed in a *certain order*. In the animated film example, storyboarding (the drawings) would be one layer in the animatic project; the editing would be another layer. These are two entirely different kinds of tasks, and since you obviously can't edit the drawings before you draw them, there's a clear order to the layers (Figure 22.4).

Chunk your project to slices when it involves *similar tasks, in arbitrary order*. In the animation film example, we've chunked the storyboard layers to sequences (Figure 22.5). Each sequence is a slice: they're all the same type of project, and the order of completion generally doesn't matter.

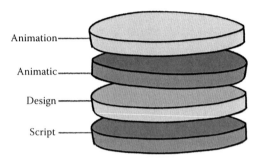

FIGURE 22.4   *The layers of our animated short production are sequential, and each requires a different skill set.*

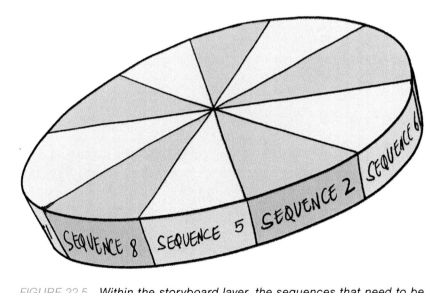

FIGURE 22.5   *Within the storyboard layer, the sequences that need to be drawn are* **slices**: *similar tasks that can be created in arbitrary order.*

Slicing is obviously great for a homogeneous team working in parallel, since the slices have independent timelines. However, slicing can also be a lifesaver when you work alone. When the amount of details in your work becomes overwhelming, chunk it to slices, and then work in passes within each slice separately. It's a very effective way of reducing complexity and regaining control.

Slices or Layers?

The choice between slicing and layering isn't always obvious. For example, suppose you're a writer, and you're working on a certain chapter in your novel. The chapter—in itself a chunk, of course— is still too overwhelming to be worked on linearly; it needs to be chunked further. But how should you chunk it? Should you work on each paragraph separately (slices)? Should you write each character separately (also slices)? Or should you focus on the plot first, then do dialogues and descriptions, then refine language and styling (layers)?

The answer is: whenever you can, always prefer layers over slices. Layers keep your mind on the big picture; slices narrow your focus and therefore put you in more danger of losing sight of what's important. You should only chunk to slices when layers don't make sense, or when you feel overwhelmed by the scope of the work.

Placeholders

Placeholders are a powerful tool that combines capturing with fractal chunking. The idea is to capture your concept or vision using a set of *subcaptures*. For example, a mobile app designer might capture his/her vision for a web page using a set of placeholders, each representing an element that is yet to be created. Designers often build a complete and functioning app (aka a premake) with nothing but placeholders, allowing them to focus on function without getting caught up in details or aesthetics (Figure 22.6).

FIGURE 22.6 *On the left: a functioning version of my mobile app AppSpace, built entirely out of placeholders. Some are crude captures to be reworked later (e.g., the buttons), others were grabbed from random sources such as old projects.*

Placeholders are widely used in creative mediums in which the final work is an arrangement of individual elements. A few examples are web and UI design (as discussed above), computer games (where each level is made of individual objects interacting with each other), and interior design (which is largely about arranging separate elements in a pleasing and practical way). In this kind of medium, placeholders are usually the fastest and most cost-effective way of creating a premake.

The reason I'm discussing placeholders here rather than in the Capture section or the premake chapter is that the idea of placeholders connects perfectly with the idea of fractal chunking. When your premake is made of a set of captured elements, the chunking process works logically with the content of the work, which makes for a smoother and more predictable workflow. On top of that, when the time comes to start working on your subprojects, these captured elements become instant premakes. This is a huge time saver, and it also helps in making sure that all the elements fit seamlessly together and work well in their context (Figure 22.7).

FIGURE 22.7 *This shot (from a short animated film) was fully prepared, animated, and edited into the film using crude placeholders. Once the big-picture issues were resolved and set, each component became the premake for a subproject, to be completed separately and then injected back into the already completed shot.*

Top to Bottom

This section is both an example and an overview of the entire subject of chunking. We're going to break down a complex project all the way from top to bottom, giving you a glimpse at how a real large-scale project might be planned and managed.

Note that this could get a bit technical, perhaps even slightly overwhelming. Don't panic; most of your projects won't require that kind of control. However, when you do find yourself in need of an extraordinary level of control, speed, and focus, remember that you have these management tools at your disposal. They have saved my creative neck more times that I can remember.

So, let's get to it. This time, I'll take designing and building a medium-sized website as our project example. Let's assume the web designer has a month to finish the project.

We'll begin, as always, with our three main stages: Concept to come up with an exciting and original design, Vision to study the concept and develop it to a full creative vision, and Production to create the actual assets for the site.

We know that, as a rule of thumb, Concept and Vision together should take about 25% of the total time. Since we have a month, a good bet would be to allocate one week for those and three weeks for the Production part (Figure 22.8).

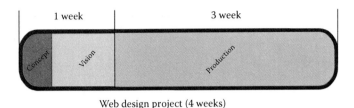

Web design project (4 weeks)

FIGURE 22.8   *Chunking the project.*

Let's fast forward: the first week is done, a premake has been created, and the designer is about to begin the Production stage. The premake indicates that the site is going to have 10 individual pages, each of which is already captured using placeholders.

What's the next chunking step?

We *could* slice it to pages and have the designer work on each page separately, but that may cause the site as a whole to feel inconsistent. Instead, let's chunk it to layers. The standard production chunks (blocking/shaping/refining) would be excellent for that purpose, giving us exactly three layers for the three weeks of Production (Figure 22.9). I'm not going to get into what each of these chunks means in terms of the web design work itself. There's no need to make this more complicated than it already is. We just need the chunking approach to be clear.

Week #1	Week #2	Week #3
Blocking	Shaping	Refining

Project > production (3 weeks)

FIGURE 22.9   *Chunking the production stage.*

We're now at the beginning of our blocking layer. We have one week to block 10 pages; that can't be a single chunk. It's too long and includes too many details. Let's zoom in and break it down further.

At this point, slicing *does* make sense: working on all the web pages at once would be needlessly confusing and overwhelming. So, we're going to slice the blocking layer to 10 slices, one for each web page, and we'll attach a timeframe to blocking each web page according to its complexity. Let's assume the homepage is by far the most demanding page in the site. We'll give it 40% of the time: assuming a five days' work week, that give us exactly two full days (Figure 22.10).

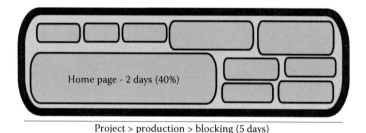

Home page - 2 days (40%)

Project > production > blocking (5 days)

FIGURE 22.10   *Slicing the blocking layer.*

We're now dealing with a pretty simple project: one focused mission (a single page that can be reviewed at a glance), two days, a single person. There is no need for more fractal chunking: this subproject can be planned and managed linearly.

We won't need a Concept stage for this project: the core concept of the homepage should already be there, captured within the site's premake. We do need a Production stage, and it also wouldn't hurt to do a bit of focused studying to solidify the vision for this very important page.

Again, let's schedule about 25% of the project (half a day) for studying, and the rest (a day and a half) will go to the Production stage.

For a two-day project, that's as far as we need to go with macro-chunking. Now, let's get efficient and add micro-deadlines to the

CAPTURE | CONCEPT | VISION | PRODUCTION |

PLAN

plan (Figure 22.11). Notice that I've only done this for day 1 for now; day 2 would be chunked to micro-deadlines after day 1 is done.

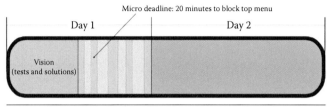

Project > production > blocking > homepage (2 days)

FIGURE 22.11   *Linear chunking of the two-days-long Home Page subproject.*

This is as far as we need to go with our extensive chunking example. I know it was a bit technical, but I hope it helped you see how chunking works. I also hope it helped you see how the idea of "structured chaos" works in practice, and how it provides a high level of control over very complex projects, while leaving lots of room for the much needed chaos of creativity.

Last Problem to Solve

With that, we're done talking about chunking. You now have all the tools you need to plan and manage any creative project, at any size or level of complexity.

Before we wrap it all up, however, there's one aspect of chunking that we haven't quite discussed yet. If your project is made of dozens of chunks, branches, sub-projects, layers and slices, how do you keep it coherent? How do you make sure it doesn't end up a mishmash of awkwardly glued-together elements?

In the next chapter, I'll present you with one last set of tools: the tools of working in context.

23

Working in Context

My first computer game animation ever was of a guard waiting near a bank entrance. He had no role in the story—just a piece of setting to make things look more real. Since it was my first task in the company, I wanted to impress them with my animation skills. I invested some real effort in that little piece of animation: my bank guard swayed back and forth with boredom, turned slowly back to check his surrounding, then got back to swaying. I refined my work and was quite pleased with the result.

Then I submitted the animation into the game…and realized for the first time that it wasn't just one guard standing there. The game level was full of them, and now they were all swaying back and forth, doing this very distinct and complex movement over and over and over again. The effect was quite surreal and, of course, very wrong.

The mistake I made was not considering the *context* of my work: the entire Romanesco Broccoli of my little branch, if you will. What the context needed was a piece of bland and unremarkable animation; what I had created was unique, interesting, and very distinct.

CAPTURE — CONCEPT — VISION — PRODUCTION

PLAN

Here's the moral of the story: as a professional creative, most of your work is going to happen within some kind of context. That context can have a significant impact on how you approach and judge your work. Part of managing and planning your projects is, therefore, to make sure that those considerations are being heeded.

That's true not only when you're working for someone else but also when you're working on your own personal project. Why are you creating this? What are you trying to say? Who's going to see the piece? What are your resources? These are all contextual considerations that should be reflected in your work. Moreover, even on your own project, most of your work is going to be a small chunk of something bigger: a shot in your film, an asset in your game, a chapter in your book, and so on. In terms of planning, this isn't any different from working for a client, except that in this case the client is yourself, which makes it even *more* critical that you to keep yourself context-aware.

In this chapter, you'll learn how to make sure your work fits right into its context—and how to use the context as a source of inspiration and focus for your work.

The 4 W's

Before you ever start working on your particular "branch" of the broccoli, your first step should be to ask yourself four questions: *what, who, when,* and *why*. This may seem too obvious to even mention, but you'll be surprised at how easily people forget to ask themselves these questions—as demonstrated in my little game animation story. Let's quickly go through them.

What Am I Creating?

This is about the content and the artistic style of the piece. Asking the *what* question will help protect you from gravitating toward your own personal style. My bank guard story is a good example of that: I used my own animation style, neglecting to consider the limited style used in the game for animating background characters.

Who Am I Creating This for?

The answer can be trickier than you think. Imagine, for example, you're doing storyboards for a video ad about car safety for kids. Here, you have at least three layers of audience to consider:

> **The commercial agency that hired you.** Do they need the boards for their own internal use, or are they going to present them to their client? This can totally change how you approach the work.

> **The clients of your client:** these are the people paying for the ad. What are they looking for? What's their message? Also, how experienced are they in seeing storyboards?

> **The actual audience of the commercial.** is this ad talking directly to the kids, or is it addressing their parents? If it's for the kids, what are *they* after? If it's for the parents, what are *they* interested in?

As you can see, the answers to those questions can completely change the way you approach the task, and have the power to make your work more valuable to both your clients and your audience.

When Do I Need to Finish It?

Taking deadlines into account is, of course, critical. Make sure you choose a concept that can be made on time and on budget, and plan your Production stage so that it aims for the appropriate level of quality. I've seen too many creatives struggle—and sometimes fail—just because they forgot to take those practical considerations into account.

Why Am Doing This?

This is perhaps the least obvious question of the four, but in terms of impact on your work, it's probably the most powerful one. Think of it this way: someone (perhaps yourself) is investing resources in doing this work. Why? Why is this particular branch of the broccoli important enough to invest resources in? How does it serve the big picture? *What would be missing if it wasn't there?*

CAPTURE | CONCEPT | VISION | PRODUCTION

PLAN

This last question is particularly revealing. For example, suppose you're a web designer, and you're currently designing the "About" page of your client's website. Why are you doing this? One possible answer would be: "well, every site has to have one, it's nothing special. I'll just block in room for some text, add a picture of the product, job done." Now let's dig deeper: "what would be missing in that site if the 'About' page wasn't there?" Looking at the context with that question in mind, suppose you notice that most of the site is pretty practical and impersonal. Maybe the About page can be a good place to inject some personality? That's an interesting thought, which translates directly to design choices: maybe there should be a photo of the staff, maybe a larger area for text to allow for a more personal message, maybe you'll use warmer colors. Whatever it is, you're now working at an entirely new level. The task became that much more interesting, and your client is going to get more than they had ever expected—all because you asked the right question.

Calibrating Your Inner Critic

When it comes to judging your work, context may sometimes completely reverse the meaning of "good" and "bad." Referring to my bank guard story again: in and of itself, bland animation is "bad" and captivating animation is "good." In the context of the game, however, they were reversed: bland animation became "good" and captivating animation became "bad."

This isn't rare at all. Working in context, you will often find yourself actively aiming for blurry, annoying, oversaturated, monotonous, or any other kind of "bad" work. Think about it as *calibrating your inner critic*: everything you know about your craft will scream at you that it's wrong, but when you work in context, *wrong* is often the *right* thing to do.

Calibrating your inner critic is not just about what's important— it's also about what's *not* important, and understanding that will often save you a lot of work.

Case in point: When I was working on *Asterix and the Vikings*, a friend of mine—a very experienced animator—once showed me a small oddity in one of his shots. In that shot, an angry guy had to walk across the frame and smash a wall. The background for the shot was drawn in such a way that the character needed to step down from the grass onto the path.

A lesser animator might have animated the character taking that step down, just to match the background. Instead, my friend *cheated*: he animated the character as if the background was completely flat. I remember his explanation word for word, because it was one of those "a-ha" moments for me. He said, "this is *not* the story about a man stepping down from the grass. This is the story about a man walking over and smashing a wall." As a seasoned professional, he was acutely aware of his context: the "why" of his work, the story his shot was there to tell. He had the confidence to make a deliberate mistake in order to prevent distraction and protect that context. Incidentally, it also considerably simplified his task.

Enhancing Your Work

Just like with scheduling and planning, some creatives don't like the idea of working in context. They feel it limits their creative freedom, and forces them to act against their creative instincts.

To counter that, I'd like to show you three ways to have the context push your creativity forward rather than inhibit it.

Use the Context for Inspiration and Originality

As a teacher, I know that the best way to build a creative block for your students is to give them a completely open task. Tell a student to "write a short horror story" and you'll get a frustrated person writing a bunch of clichés. Now, throw in a couple of completely random restrictions, such as "write a short horror story, two pages long, and it has to include a typewriter and an axe," and the creative juices start flowing. In fact, I'll bet some part of your mind is already busy working out that story right now. Am I right?

CAPTURE | CONCEPT | VISION | PRODUCTION

PLAN

The point is that restrictions are an excellent source of creativity and inspiration. As a professional creative, you don't have a teacher to create random restrictions for you; but you *do* have the context. Make a special effort to find helpful restrictions in the context. The more outrageous, specific, and uncomfortable those restrictions are, the more unique your work is going to be. That's because you'll be forced to abandon your regular go-to solutions and come up with new and unexpected ideas.

Use the Context to Keep Things Simple

When it comes to creative work, simple isn't simple at all. Making something simple that is also unique and interesting is a very difficult trick to pull.

As it turns out, you can actually use the context to help simplify your work. Let me show you how. Look at the spot in Figure 23.1.

●

FIGURE 23.1 *A spot.*

Any idea what this is supposed to be? No, of course not. It's just a spot, right? But how about if I add some context around it, as in Figure 23.2?

FIGURE 23.2 *Smiley.*

Notice that I have just turned a meaningless spot into an eye—a very intricate organ, by the way—*without ever changing the actual spot.* In fact, it's not just that spot: the entire "face" is made of a bunch of shapes that give meaning to each other, but are meaningless outside that context.

This is a simplified visualization of a strong creative tool: you can simplify your work to a huge degree by relying on the context to do the heavy "explaining." In fact, if *don't* do it, you may end up with a very weird result (Figure 23.3).

FIGURE 23.3   *Weird smiley.*

Once again, my gaming guard animation makes a great example. When you have a guy in a guard uniform outside a bank, you don't really need the whole "look at me I'm a guard" animation for people to understand what this guy is doing. All you need to do is support what they've already deduced. Since I was working out of context, without the background and with a simplified representation of the character that did not include the uniform, I subconsciously took it upon my animation to explain the entire situation. That, of course, was the wrong thing to do.

Use the Context to Gain Creative Freedom

The context's influence on meaning is so strong, that you can often completely switch the content with something entirely different and the audience will still get it.

In Figure 23.4, are those eyes or shells? I guess they're both. This demonstrates how you can use context to think outside the box and add something unexpected to your work: a cute twist, a little oddity,

FIGURE 23.4 *"Shell eyes."*

maybe a clever metaphor ("shell eyes!"). Or, you can just use it as an opportunity to add extra richness to your work without confusing your audience. As long as it sits well within the context, it will hold.

As a concrete example, think of a character in a film. In the previous scene, she and her friend had a serious car crash. Now she's at the graveyard. It's raining. The soundtrack is slow and mournful. All those elements act exactly like the different parts of the smiley: in and of themselves, they don't mean much—but together, they tell the story perfectly. Do you need a line of dialogue to know what happened? Do you need the character to do a sad face or sob? I don't think so. She could just stand there, and her sadness will be as clear as the smiley's eye.

Then again, instead of just standing there, she could take a shell out her pocket and put it gently on the grave. And now it's interesting. Now, there's something there beyond the sadness: a story that's waiting to be told.

To conclude, understanding your context is important, not just as a way of making sure your branch of the broccoli works well within the bigger broccoli, but also as a way of making your work richer, simpler, and more interesting.

Elevating Your Context

So far, we've discussed two levels of context awareness: the "let's not break the context" level, and the more advanced "let's use the context to our advantage" level. Now let's discuss a third level of context awareness: elevating your context. That means that you don't just make sure your work fits seamlessly into the bigger broccoli. You take it upon yourself to actually make the broccoli better.

This higher level of context awareness often comes from answering the *WHY* question. Remember the web design example, in which we used the "About" page to add a personal touch to the website? That was an example of using a subproject in a way that elevates the whole.

Figure 23.5 shows another example. This famous etching by Gustave Dore tells a very clear story: the innocent Abel was killed by Cain in a fit of rage.

FIGURE 23.5   *Cain and Abel.*

Notice how every single element of the work is designed to tell this story: the twisted vegetation, the black angry sky, the bent silhouette of Cain—not at all happy and victorious, but suffering and lost, his beard as tangled as his thoughts, and on the ground—Abel, spread eagled, his face as smooth as that of an innocent child.

All these different "branches" of the broccoli are shaped by the intended message of the work—the "fit of rage" story—and they in turn help to shape that message.

What makes this work a masterpiece is not just the superb level of craftsmanship, but also the ability to use context in a sophisticated way to tell the story from that specific point of view (which is entirely an artistic interpretation, by the way, because in the Bible, there's no mention of an uncontrolled fit of rage).

But then, of course, this "broccoli" isn't a broccoli at all. It's just a branch in a much bigger broccoli: Gustave Dore's illustrated Bible project (*La Grande Bible de Tours*), which includes 241 wood engravings, every one of them as wonderful as this one. The choice of giving the story that particular interpretation is just another way of enriching and enhancing that greater broccoli.

And with that, we have come full circle—all the way back to that structure of art-within-art-within-art or workflow-within-workflow-within-workflow; and hopefully you can now see just how big and complex this structure can be, and how being good at working within your context is the glue that holds this whole structure together as a coherent and satisfying work of art.

CAPTURE — CONCEPT — VISION — PRODUCTION — PLAN

Conclusion

This concludes our discussion about chunking and project management.

We've learned how to chunk a simple project linearly, to seven standard macro-chunks, and how to chunk it further to micro-deadlines that keep you focused and effective. We then discussed the idea of chunking a project into subprojects, applying the same Concept–Vision–Production workflow to each subproject, and working in context to make sure it all fits together.

This is a powerful set of tools, and once you get used to them, they can help you get on top of any project that comes your way. It's worth mentioning, though, that in most situations you won't need to use this full set of management tools. When it comes down to it, the one planning habit I advise you to keep in mind and practice regularly is this: spend 15 minutes every day—preferably first thing in the morning—planning ahead and giving yourself time-specific tasks for the next couple of days. In 9 out of 10 projects, this will be enough to eliminate much of the stress inherent in creative work, and to put you in control of the situation.

Most importantly, I hope I've been able to show you that at its best, planning and managing do not contradict creativity. On the contrary: they enhance it, adding thrust and rhythm to your work, creating confidence, and focusing your efforts. It is an integral part of the exciting challenge that is being a professional creative.

AT A GLANCE:

THE PLAN

Chunk your project down
to short, hyper-focused creative bursts

PLANNING AND MANAGING DON'T IMPAIR YOUR CREATIVITY. THEY PROTECT IT.

LINEAR CHUNKING
BREAKING DOWN A SIMPLE PROJECT

THE 7 STANDARD CHUNKS:
CONCEPT | DRY STUDY | WET STUDY | PREMAKE | BLOCKING | SHAPING | REFINING

MICRO DEADLINES: SHORT HYPER-FOCUSED BURSTS
ADAPTIVE PLANNING: KEEP CHUNKING AS YOU GO

FRACTAL CHUNKING
BREAKING DOWN A LARGE/COMPLEX PROJECT

LAYERS: DISSIMILAR TASKS IN LOGICAL ORDER
SLICES: SIMILAR CHUNKS IN RANDOM ORDER
PLACEHOLDERS: A CAPTURE MADE OF SUB-CAPTURES

WORKING IN CONTEXT
FITTING YOUR CHUNK INTO THE WHOLE

THE 4 W'S: WHAT? WHO? WHEN? WHY?
USE THE CONTEXT FOR:
INSPIRATION, SIMPLICITY, CREATIVE FREEDOM
HOW CAN YOU USE YOUR WORK TO ENHANCE THE BIGGER PICTURE?

Section VII

A CASE STUDY

"It felt as though I was carving a book out of this
mess of notes. And that's in effect what I did. It was
a question of condensing, and editing, and sculpting a book out of this mass of stuff that I had on
Harry."

J.K. Rowling

This section contains a commentated case study of creative workflow, from start to finish, prepared especially for this book.

We're going to write together an adaptation of the story of Little Red Riding Hood. I chose that as a starting point because we all know the story, and because it's been adapted so many times before that it makes an interesting challenge for our new workflow: can we use the principles presented in this book to freshen up this very familiar tale, and to make it feel new and exciting?

The reason I chose writing as a medium is that it provides a simple and straightforward way to add comments and thoughts as I go along. It is also the most widely accessible creative medium.

From this point on, you're reading my work as it happened, with almost no editing involved. I've even left some spelling and grammar mistakes untouched so that you can feel the pure stream of thoughts and how they slowly evolve into the finished text.

Formatting note: The text marked yellow is workflow notes added during the process of writing. Everything written in boxes is workflow comments I've added after the fact.

Here goes…

Chapter 24

Before We Begin: Analyzing Context

Every creative project (or sub-project) should start with a deep look into the *context*. What am I aiming for? What is the purpose of this? What are the limitations? Who's reading this?

First, I need to get my bearings here. Where am I going with this? I'll start with breaking down the original Little Red Riding Hood (LRRH) story to five parts:

1. Mom sends LRRH to grandma (through forest).

2. LRRH meets wolf, tells him about grandma.

3. Wolf eats grandma and waits in bed.

4. LRRH talks to wolf thinking it's grandma, gets eaten as well.

5. Hunter gets to hut, saves both LRRH and grandma.

Doing the entire thing is out of the scope of this exercise, so I'll focus just on part 2: "LRRH meets wolf, tells him about grandma." This part just feels the most interesting to me.

Now I know *what* I'm doing. Of course, part of analyzing the context of the work is figuring out *why* I'm doing it and how this is going to affect my work.

Since the whole point is to show how the creative process works, I shouldn't turn the whole thing into a big joke or completely reinvent the story. I'm thinking of making this a bit of a "Harry Potter" sort of thing—make it less absurd and more lifelike, plus a maybe bit magical. I'd also like to give the characters an interesting personality.

Some other creative constraints I can find in the context are as follows:

- I know that everyone knows the story. I should try and use that; rely on it to some extent, maybe plant some subtle jokes based on that.

- Part 2 is the only part of the story that takes place in the forest. So, part of the fun would be to take the reader into this great fantasy forest, as charming as it gets and also as dangerous and as wild as it gets.

Already at this point, just by looking at the context, I have a clear and quite interesting framework to work within.

Let's summarize what we have so far:

1. LRRH meets wolf, tells him about grandma.

2. Charming + dangerous forest scenery should be prominent.

3. Interesting personalities for the characters.

4. Add a flavor of a magical fantasy world.

With that framework in mind, we're off to the Concept stage.

Chapter **25**

Stage I: Concept

Step 1: Raw Materials

As we know, the first step in coming up with a concept is to pour out many raw ideas. They don't have to be good or anything, just raw materials we can build a concept with.

I start with asking myself why LRRH would leave the safe path and go wandering off into the forest. Maybe she chases a butterfly and loses track? This would make her a dreamy, absent-minded kind of girl.

So maybe something like the following:

- LRRH happy in forest
- Chases butterfly, not noticing she's off path
- Tries to return to path—feels like someone's following her; panicking
- LRRH realizes she's completely lost, starts crying
- Wolf reveals himself, talks to her, learns about grandma

> Notice the brief writing, with simple grammar and abbreviations. Speed plays a part when it comes to capturing.
>
> *Dry capturing* allows faster reading. This is important because later we'll want to review the ideas quickly and see what we can make of them. Long *wet-capturing* style paragraphs will make that more difficult.

My first idea—LRRH chases a butterfly off the path—quickly grew into a concept, which is actually pretty good, I think. It certainly works within the context. This is, however, just my first idea, so I'll want to keep on pouring stuff out—I have no intention of falling into the "first concept trap."

A few more reasons LRRH would go off path can be:

- Maybe she just doesn't care; she doesn't even believe in wolves.

- Maybe she's curious about something and goes checking.

- What if she falls off the path somehow? Maybe it's hard to climb back?

- Maybe she can't climb back because she's hurt; maybe she twisted her ankle.

- There's a sudden mist and she got lost.

- What if it starts raining and she's deep in the forest?

- The weather changes and it turns the forest from charming to menacing.

At this point, I find it hard to continue; I hit a bit of a dead end. I'll try to *break my thinking pattern* by doing something else and changing my train of thought—how about telling the story from the wolf's point of view?

- Wolf in forest, hungry and angry.

- Maybe his prey got away at the last moment (up the stakes!).

- Hunter got to it first…
- Maybe wolf is just about to succeed and LRRH ruins it.
- What if he pounces on her and she runs away?
- Maybe he's about to pounce but hunter saves her at the very last moment?
- How does he learn about grandma? Maybe LRRH talks to herself and he hears her?
- Maybe she called grandma on the cellphone and wolf overhears. << YES it's a silly idea—Getting silly is a great pattern breaker!

At this point, I already feel how some of my raw ideas naturally connect with each other, and I can see some vague opportunities for concepts. I'll go for it:

Concept 2 << The first one was the one with LRRH as a dreamy girl

- Wolf in forest, hungry, angry, lost his prey because of hunter.
- Suddenly spots LRRH lost in forest. Follows her.
- Almost attacks, but then suddenly she bumps into hunter. Wolf lost again!
- LRRH tells hunter about grandma, wolf overhears, goes for grandma.

This is a pretty neat version! Here's another one:

Concept 3

- Wolf hunting.
- LRRH, happy and oblivious, makes prey run away.
- Wolf furious but LRRH doesn't notice, she's a talkative air-head; says she's going to grandma.
- Wolf becomes interested, asks directions, says bye politely, and goes off to "see" grandma.

This makes me think of a new direction: what if the wolf is actually *looking* for grandma? Like it's been his life's ambition to attack this woman? Maybe he realizes this is a great opportunity to get past her defenses (whatever they are) by impersonating LRRH? << Yeah, that's pretty silly too.

Scanning my ideas, I feel there's something interesting about LRRH not believing there's a wolf. This connects to the magical/fantasy/mythical feel I was going for. I'd like to try a few ideas in that direction.

- Is the wolf a mythical creature? A mysterious bigfoot-like creature?
- Maybe there are legends of "the wolf" and all the villagers are afraid of him.
- LRRH is terrified of the wolf; has nightmares.
- But mom says it's all just ignorant superstition, and that's why she sends LRRH alone to the forest. << Great opportunity for conflict!

Notice how:

- Analyzing the *context* makes a difference, by keeping me alert to a certain type of ideas (in this case, the magical/fantasy/mythical type).
- You can nudge your brain to explore more ideas in a certain area, but without constraining it too much.

Concept 4

Context: big conflict in part 1 where mom sends LRRH into forest even though she's terrified.

- LRRH in forest, terrified, keeps to the path.
- A small animal makes her panic and run for it.
- Trying to get back to path but getting lost.

- Meets wolf but doesn't recognize him as the wolf.
- Wolf helps her get back to path…and goes for grandma.

> This is a typical "inspiration moment": a simple idea that builds quickly into a full concept.
>
> Whether we'll use this idea or not—notice how quickly the Concept process creates "inspiration conditions."

Concept 4 made me think of the wolf as spooky—maybe some kind of a ghost or a demon (another raw idea to play with). This opens up a new and very promising thinking pattern, but I feel I have enough to work with right now. I'm dropping it to avoid the confusing "too many options" pitfall.

I want to explore one more possibility—that LRRH is a curious kid that's more fascinated with the wolf myth than she is afraid of it. This feels like a more likable character.

Concept 5

- LRRH in forest, very curious about everything.
- Sees something; decides to explore, very carefully.
- Slips and falls; suddenly a new interesting world opens up.
- Explores wonderful forest; finds interesting cave.
- It's the wolf's cave; he attacks her.
- She tells about grandma, wolf releases her, goes to grandma.

> I keep using my raw ideas as building blocks for these concepts. The "slip and fall," for example, came up as a raw idea in the beginning of the brainstorm process.

The cave idea made me think that maybe it's a she-wolf? Maybe she has wolf-cubs to feed? This will make her a villain with a worthy cause. I like that.

At this stage, I feel I have enough to work with. However, for the sake of making the example more complete, I want to use a few more pattern breaking techniques.

I start by looking at images of forests. One of the first images shows the point where two forest paths cross—didn't think about that at all! My hidden pattern was "there is a single path through the forest all the way to grandma's house."

Let's come up with some crossroad ideas:

- LRRH gets to crossroad. Sign fell. She has to guess where to go—chooses wrong!

- Wolf deliberately changes the sign to confuse her (like in cartoons…).

- Mom says "turn right" but she forgets and goes left.

A few images later, another pattern is broken: in my head, a path was something very clear. But the images remind me that paths in a real forest are nothing like paths in city parks. They're often very confusing. Something that looks like a path could easily become a dead-end after a while or disappear and leave you completely lost.

This leads to the following option: << This isn't a full concept, just a more detailed dry capture of a raw idea.

- LRRH afraid, sticks to path.

- Makes a wrong decision—goes into a natural path that goes into forest.

- Forest becomes more and more dense and disturbing.

- Is something following her?! Walks faster.

- Path gradually getting less clear—now she can't figure out how to get back.

The crossroad and the disappearing path are classic pattern breaking examples. In both cases, I had no idea of how oversimplified my notion of a path had been. Only when I broke out of the pattern could I see how it limited my thinking. You can have a strong pattern that makes zero sense: a long forest path that leads exclusively to grandma's house with no crossroads? Really?

Until now, I've only done *dry capturing*: factual, editable, bulleted lists, cutting my ideas to smaller pieces. I'll do a quick *wet capture* now and see where that takes me.

Concept 6—wet capture:

LRRH happy in forest, picks flowers, mushrooms. Feels real hungry. Eats mushroom. Feels much better—forest becomes so colorful, animals move slowly, sounds become sweeter. Maybe she hears music...? Walks into forest, enchanted, forgets herself and about the wolf and everything else. Maybe follows a *huge* butterfly. Maybe it speaks to her.

She's deep in the forest when things start shifting—forest becomes darker, mysterious, haunted. Because of the mushrooms, everything is sharper, louder, bigger, more extraordinary. Plants look like skulls and sounds become screechy and disturbing.

Meanwhile...wolf is nearby, forest is normal of course—he knows it well. Sees footsteps (maybe something she dropped?). Gets curious, follows. Sniffs. Gets closer and closer. He's very hungry—we know she's in a real danger. He sees her and she sees him but then she comes to him happily, starts talking to him. "Sir...I'm lost, I need to get to grandma." She thinks he's a person. Wolf is amazed that he can actually understand her speech! Starts asking about grandma, licks his lips—he's going to have one great meal today! Now he knows all and gets ready to eat LRRH and get to grandma when suddenly, hunter interrupts, and he runs away. Hunter escorts LRRH to path.

Notice:

- The natural flow of events in a wet capture, and how rich and sensual it feels.

- The disadvantages of wet capturing: hard to scan, hard to edit, and the details obscure the structure.

- Even though this capture is more detailed than the previous ones, the focus here is not on the details but on the more abstract aspects of the scene: mood, emotions, flow. The specific details are just instruments and can easily be changed later.

Step 2: Forming Concepts

At this point, I feel I have enough raw material to work with. In fact, I already have some initial concepts that just "happened" along the way during the first step (which is not unusual but also not mandatory—it's fine to end step 1 with just a bunch of ideas). I can certainly feel these ideas itching to connect, and I'm excited to start playing around with them and see what happens.

As I go over the different ideas and concepts, I like how in concepts 4 and 6 we know she's in real danger even though she doesn't realize it yet. The beginning of those versions is strong but the ending is weak. How about this:

Concept 7

(Context: big conflict in part 1—mom sends LRRH into forest even though she's terrified).

- LRRH in forest, terrified, keeps to the path.

- A small animal makes her panic and run for it.

- Trying to get back to path but getting lost.

- Meets wolf but doesn't recognize him as the wolf. Tells him about grandma.

- Wolf is about to attack—hears the hunter—quietly disappears and heads to grandma.

Here's another thought: Concept 5 is great in that LRRH has an appealing and energetic personality, which could contrast nicely with a stern mom. The ending is again weak, but concept 3 offers a good alternative. In addition, the fading/unclear forest paths idea can strengthen the beginning. The resulting concept:

Concept 8

- LRRH in the forest; very curious about everything.

- Takes a "fake path" by mistake, the forest gets even more interesting.

- Hears some noises—what could that be?

- A big boar! Slips and falls away from fake path.

- Finds herself in a wonderful and charming place.

- Wolf is hunting. He's not really a wolf, but a mythical being—somewhere between animal and human.

- Happy and oblivious, LRRH scares away a wonderful tasty deer.

- Wolf is furious. Follows her a little. She's in great danger.

- Just before he attacks, the hunter finds her. She tells him about grandma.

- Wolf, even more hungry, even more furious, goes off to find grandma.

Concept 8 is a great example of how raw ideas and half-baked concepts serve as building blocks for a strong concept. At least five different ideas have been used to build this one.

Step 3: The Final Concept

I now have two "mature" concepts (#7 and #8), and I feel very much ready to choose.

I had let it rest for a day or so to be able to judge the concepts more clearly. I've also shown these ideas to a colleague. We both agreed that concept 8 is clearly superior. It has everything the context analysis had suggested: the forest scenery that turns from charming to dangerous, interesting personalities, and a flavor of myth and fantasy. It also has a good emotional landscape—fear, exuberance, fury. This is the concept we'll be working with.

The final act of this stage is to capture the emotional core of the concept. I'll switch from dry to wet and capture what I feel is really exciting about this concept:

Final Concept

Little Red Riding Hood is excited (and anxious) about being all alone in the great forest for the first time.

After a quick, confusing chain of events, she finds herself deep in the forest. She's lost, but charmed out of her fears by the wild beauty of the place.

Then the scene turns ominous as the hungry and angry mythical "wolf" prepares to make her his next meal.

This is going to be our concept, and I hope you like it. I'm super excited about it—can't wait to start developing it into a full vision!

Chapter 26

Stage II: Vision

The Dry Study

Building a vision is all about getting more familiar with your materials—in this case, the plot, the characters, and the setting.

When I think of what I *don't* know, the first thing that comes to mind is just the rest of the story. What happens before LRRH goes into the forest? What happens after the wolf leaves?

So, my first *dry study* step is to write an outline of the full story—just so I can have the full picture in my mind. I'm sure having that context in mind will inform what I'm doing in many ways.

1. Mom sends LRRH to forest

   - LRRH plays with younger brother; she plays the wolf.

   - Mom—owner of village inn—rebukes her: there's no "big bad wolf."

   - Hunter happens to be in the inn; says there *is*—he's seen it.

- Heated argument between mom and hunter; also argue about grandma living in forest.

- Mom sends LRRH to bring grandma food—for the first time alone. LRRH is excited.

- Outside, mom warns LRRH to not stray from the path. LRRH promised to do that.

2. LRRH meets wolf, tells him about grandma

- LRRH in forest; path boring, forest fascinating.

- Curiosity tempts LRRH to take just a few steps off the path.

- Slips; basket rolls down the hill, she goes to fetch it.

- Finds herself in awe-inspiring wild forest.

- Unknowingly causes wolf to lose his prey.

- Angry, he follows her. He's mean; has a sadistic side.

- LRRH feels someone's following her. Suddenly the forest feels ominous.

- Just as the wolf is about to attack, the hunter from the village appears; saves her.

- They talk about grandma and where she is. Wolf overhears, and goes looking for her.

3. Wolf attacks grandma

- Wolf arrives at grandma's house; it is fortified and secure.

- Uses something the hunter said to get her to open door.

- He pounces!

4. Wolf gets LRRH too

- LRRH and hunter arrive at grandma's; part ways.

- LRRH enters house. Why is door open? (tension builds)

- Finds the wolf dressed as grandma in bed. They talk (more or less the famous dialogue from the original tale).

- Pounces; LRRH gives a good fight, almost succeeds in escaping.

- Wolf finally catches her; puts her in room where grandma is held (maybe he wanted to hurt her before eating her…?)

- Advances on both of them. All is lost.

5. Hunter saves the day

- Hunter suddenly burst into house; epic fight with wolf.

- LRRH gets free; helps hunter win (using a trick from her game with her brother in Part 1).

- Hunter explains why he's back; he noticed something was wrong.

- Back to village, with wolf tied up and beaten. Village astonished. Mom admits her mistake; hugs LRRH and grandma. Grandma decides to come back and live in the village.

- LRRH and hunter are the big heroes of the day— become good friends.

Okay, that feels good enough. I now have that sense of confidence that comes from knowing where I'm at.

Sequence 2—the one I'm actually working on—involves LRRH, the wolf, the hunter, and several areas of the forest. I really don't know much about those elements. Have I ever written anything that takes place in a fantasy forest? No. Do I walk in amazing forests on regular basis? Nope. Do I even write fiction regularly? Also, no. What season are we at? Who is the hunter and what is he like? What's the deal with the wolf? LRRH is just *slightly* more defined, but even she is still more of a general idea than a full-fledged character.

So, let's start studying. I'm going to build up some general information about LRRH's world, starting with the basics:

- Season: beginning of autumn. Many trees still green, but some red around green leaves, and some trees already quite red. Quite cold; need a coat. Ground is moist; it rained a few days ago.

- We're in northern Europe (perhaps Sweden?).

- Time of day: we start around 10 a.m. and end around noon (I want them back at the village early evening).

- Characters: LRRH is a cute girl, 10 years old, fair hair. The hunter is 40 years old, strong, tall, a bit ungainly, a bit of "beer belly" in the making. The wolf is a weird mix of a real wolf and a dangerous outlaw that lives in the woods.

One of the things I wanted from the get-go is for the forest to be a big part of the sequence. So, I look for images of a Swedish forest, capturing them with words:

- Huge trees, lots of moss on barks, branches, rocks, earth.

- Mushrooms everywhere—many kinds, many sizes.

- Tall, airy, feels like a cathedral. << Notice the wet-capture ("reminds me of")

- Ground is very brown.

- Soft light coming through the trees; kind of yellowish.

- Very light fog—gives everything a more charming, mysterious feel.

- Air is clear, "crispy," refreshing. Quite cold but not unpleasant.

- Not flat—hilly, many different levels, so both roots and branches are often at eye level.

- Really big boulders scattered around.

- South-east Sweden: the forest is full of lakes, from tiny to huge.

Instead of just printing or storing the images I found, I've captured then with words (the medium of this exercise). That means I'm taking only what I need and that I'm already adapting that information to fit the story and the medium.

Okay, I feel good about the general geography. Now to explore the specific locations in which the story takes place: the path, the magical wild forest area, the scary part.

The Path

The path starts at the village and enters the forest. It's not the main entrance to the village, of course: you walk between some of the small houses at the end of the village, and you get to an old rusty gate behind the woodcutter's hut. After the gate, there is a section with trees on one side and crops on the other and then you go into the forest itself. At first, there aren't so many trees and the path is clear, but after a five-minute walk the trees become bigger and denser, the path becomes darker, and now the path is but a guest in mother nature's wilderness. Birds chirp loudly, and as you walk, you sometimes hear a bush rustle as an animal of some unknown size scurries away. Occasionally, a squirrel crosses the path. A dark-colored bird with a very colorful chest bounces around on the path, rooting a bit, and then flies away.

The trees around the path are relatively young; there is a high turnover of trees in this area, probably because it's easier to cut the trees that are near the trail. The path itself is therefore quite bright and nicely lit; but just a few yards away from the path, the forest is dense, dark, and quite mysterious.

The scents of the forest are many, and change frequently. The dominant smell is of course that of the big conifers, along with the fresh smell of the damp earth from last night's rain. Here and there, a particularly fragrant herb takes over for a moment, and then dissipates again.

Occasionally you can see a butterfly sitting on a flower or a rock for a few seconds, then it flies off. Most of them are green-yellow, some are white.

The path winds leisurely through the trees for a mile or so, reaches a small stream, turns left and follows it. There are more rocks in this part, and the trees are older and more massive. The constant sound of the stream, along with sound of frogs, join the pleasant blend of forest sounds.

Much smaller paths fork out of the main path every now and again, and enter deep into the forest. Those are not human trails; they are made and used exclusively by animals.

The stream cascades gently into a tiny lake, elliptical in shape, around 50 yards in diameter. On the right, a large rock formation hangs over the lake. The path runs around the lake and continues along the stream.

Half way to grandma, the path widens before reaching a large clearing with an old abandoned cabin. A hermit lived here until he disappeared one day; no one knows what happened to him. The mysterious disappearance remains a constant source of rumors and superstitions for the villagers. This happened 10 years ago and no one had come to live there instead. No one, that is, except for hundreds of small animals and cheerful birds nesting in every available nook. The forest has claimed the house for its own.

A little further on, the trail crosses the stream on a crooked, moss-stricken and quite dilapidated bridge, and starts to climb up a relatively steep hill. This is the more difficult section of the trail: it winds between ancient trees, over boulders, occasionally disappearing for a few yards, then re-emerging. To someone not already familiar with it, losing the trail is all too easy. This continues for a good half-mile or so, after which the terrain gets milder and the trail becomes relaxed and pleasant again. The forest is exceptionally quiet around here and possesses a certain special splendor. At the top of a hill, the path finally meets grandma's cottage.

I chose wet capturing because I wanted to start feeling the details.

This feels good enough to me. I imagine LRRH will go through only a small section of the path before leaving it and going into the thick of the forest. The hermit's hut probably won't be part of the story at all, although I'm almost sure I'll have the hunter mentioning it at some point in his argument with the mom.

Writing this wet capture took about half an hour.

* * *

The next location I want to know something about is the area off the path: the deep wild forest. I want to explore it twice—once as a magical, beautiful place, and again as a shadowy and scary environment. This is going to be a dry capture, just to keep it balanced.

Wild forest as magical:

- A huge, impressive tree, trunk painted green with moss, the lower branches so large they're seated on the ground (like the tree in Østre Anlæg park in Copenhagen).

- Mushrooms of all sizes and shapes.

- Huge butterflies, much more impressive than the ones you get to see on the path.

- Two squirrels chasing each other.

- A doe passes through, then runs off.

- A constant but gentle shower of leaves, sparkling as they catch pieces of sun, creating an enchanted effect. Occasionally a short breeze intensifies the effect for a few seconds.

- Rays of light penetrating through the dense growth—the morning mist turns them into "fingers of sunlight."
- A sparkling bug walking on a branch.
- Beautifully symmetrical spider webs hanging between branches, as if in midair, holding the morning dew.
- Big rock, looks like a massive table (maybe she eats some of grandma's food?).
- Curious squirrel—she feeds it—maybe she imagines it speaking to her.
- Raccoon washing its face in a little pond.
- Snails (after the rain).
- Small lake with a little "island." Heron on island. Frog jumps into water.
- Huge leaves, some of them conspicuously nibbled by bugs.
- A large fallen tree hanging over the water (she could carefully walk over it to get to the little island).

Wild forest as ominous:

- Dark; light yet palpable fog.
- Animals flee. Heron makes loud noise of water and flapping wings. Squirrel runs up tree and disappears.
- Sound of something big stepping on dry leaves behind some trees.
- Very limited visibility, can't see far—trees in the way.
- Extreme quiet. Even the frogs stop croaking. Small noises like creaking of branches get strangely amplified.
- Very high canopy of leaves; feeling small and lonely; like being alone in a church.
- Nowhere to hide—no bushes, only tall trees you can't climb.
- Sudden loud noise from above; many birds taking off at the same time.

- Fog gets denser; clouds block the sun; suddenly feels dark and grey.
- Everything in every direction looks the same, monotonous, uniform; like a maze.
- Distant trees create scary shapes in the fog.
- Shouting for help, but the forest swallows it; she can hardly hear it herself.

I'm getting the idea to explore another point of view of the forest—that of the wolf.

Forest from the wolf's point of view:

- Knows the forest like the back of his paw—has his own names for places, e.g., "the great tree," "the pigs trail," etc.
- The smells are very strong, especially the human child's. Also the smell of the doe he's preying on.
- Imagines himself devouring the doe, sinks his teeth into the flesh. There is a strong sadistic element in his mentality.
- Notices the child from a long way away (maybe from above—some kind of hill?). Doesn't have to go to her—He knows the path will bring her to him.
- She feels like candy to him.
- Has excellent hearing—the forest tells him what's happening. By the sounds of the steps, he knows where she's going and how fast she'll get there.
- Knows many shortcuts to help him move around faster.
- The way he moves through the forest is a mix between human and animal (same goes for his way of thinking).
- Coming down a steep hill, from the big boulder down to a fallen tree trunk, walks along the trunk, then hops down to land softly on some rocks, effortlessly walks down the rock, naturally placing hands and feet at exactly the right spots. Then another soft landing, he's down. The whole thing takes seconds; he almost "flows" down, like a kind of slow parkour.

Notice that:

- Some of these bullet points are wet captures. This is a good example of *clustering*—the wet/dry synergy technique of using a *dry set of wet captures*. This gets me the best of both worlds: the simplicity and clarity of *dry capturing*, along with the emotional impact of *wet capturing*.

- I've used abbreviated writing in some of the bullet points. Not pretty, but very easy to write and, later, to read.

This feels like a good place to *switch mediums* and add some visuals to my dry study. Figure 26.1 shows a few inspiring photos, along with some doodles I made.

FIGURE 26.1   *Visual dry study.*

I'm starting to feel I'm getting familiar with this setting. I have a lot of juicy materials here to improvise with as I write, and my vision is growing richer, clearer, and more solid. This feels great!

* * *

I now want to turn my attention from the *external* world to the characters' *inner* world. I decide my next step would be to write a short monologue for each character. This'll help me get to know their point of view and their inner voice.

LRRH Monologue

(A bit of a hyperactive girl; very energetic, speaks almost without pause for breath)

"I really didn't mean to get to the middle of the forest, honestly! But then I suddenly saw the wolf, I mean I thought I saw the wolf, and then I tripped over that thing and grandma's basket fell and rolled down the hill, and I just went to get it and I was going to get right back to the path, because grandma's waiting you know, and everything was so pretty!

"There was a huge tree, I've never seen such a tree, and it had all those squirrels, and the smallest one came close and smelled the basket, and he was soooo cuuutte! And there was a lake, and a stream you can dip your feet in, in summer I mean, now it's too cold for that and also I had to get to grandma, so I just gave the little squirrel a little something and I was going to leave, but then a doe came out of the woods with her little son, and came to drink water from the lake, and they looked at me and they weren't afraid at all! I wanted to pet them but they got scared and ran off, and they scared all the animals, I don't know why they all got scared, and even my squirrel ran up the tree, and all of a sudden it was really quiet and I felt like, you know, like I was all alone in the forest.

"It was really weird, even the sun disappeared and it got a bit dark, and a little foggy, and I decided to go straight to grandma because I was getting scared, only a bit, but it really was weird how all the animals disappeared like that. And I was going towards the path, I mean I thought I was going there but I got it wrong, even though I was sure I was getting it right, and I climbed up the hill a little and the trees started getting in the way, and then I already realized I was lost, so I tried to get back to the lake but I wasn't sure about the direction, exactly.

"And then I thought I saw something big moving behind the trees, and I got really scared, and I was also scared I wouldn't be able to find the path again and then I'll have to live in the forest, and they'll only find me years later, and I thought about how mom would be so sad and think I was dead, right? So, I started crying and yelling for help but that just scared me even more because it made me feel so small, so I stopped. And then there was a lot of noise and Will the hunter showed up, and oh boy was I glad to see HIM!

"And I jumped up and hugged him hard and I think I was still crying, and he was really angry because I was in the forest all alone and not on the path, but Mr. Will is always angry anyway so it wasn't so awful. And then I told him about grandma, so he started to talk about the wolf, and said mom shouldn't send me alone to a forest that has a wolf, and I was glad mom wasn't there because every time he starts talking about the wolf, mom gets annoyed and starts saying there's no wolf in the forest and then they always start arguing.

"But mom wasn't there and Mr. Will told me stories about the wolf the whole way to grandma's. He said he saw the wolf and that it wasn't just people imagining things, there really IS a wolf! And I believe him because he walks in the forest all the time and mom just stays at the inn and cooks, so who would know better if the was a wolf? But don't tell her I said so. Mom always thinks she knows everything better than everyone."

———————————————————————————

Wolf Monologue

(A low, rasping voice, slow, a bit confused, speaking is not his thing. Does not control language very well.)

"The girl looked very cute. Very cute. Tasted a child once, it was many years ago. Yes, many years ago, hmm. Was delicious, very delicious. I don't think I killed it, maybe found it in the woods, dead. Don't remember. Maybe I killed it.

"I was tracking doe. Deer get you both lunch and dinner, very tasty. She had a baby. Small deer is delicious. I wanted both, waiting them to come to the swine path, can't escape. Then I smelled the girl. There is a strong smell of humans, yes, very strong. She ruined everything, scared them off. People are always ruining, interrupting. Should have grabbed her, but wait, maybe more people will come. I don't like people. They make trouble. They have no senses.

"The girl was alone. It smelled good, sweet, soft like that, hmm. Yes, she smelled good. She was alone. I had to grab her straight, but I was curious, she was funny, different. Not like an animal. Animals have senses. Even small deer knows you should listen to the forest. People are not listening. Funny.

"Don't know why I didn't smell the big. Maybe I was too hungry for the girl…the smell was very strong. I was hungry. Then came the big. He made a noise. He is different. It has senses, yes. I think he knew I was there. But the girl did not know. The girl said the old woman lived in the woods, on the other side. I don't go there a lot. But I'm hungry, yes, very hungry…No deer and no baby deer, so there will be old woman and girl. First to the old woman, then girl arrives for dessert, hmm hmm *(this is somewhere between a laughter and a growl)*."

At this point, it's becoming clear that the story is evolving into something I was not expecting. I had imagined a light-hearted story, maybe even silly; instead, this is becoming a bit surreal and quite dark. Should I pull back?

I read my concept capture again—I'm still on track. I consider the context of the work and decide I don't want to force it to be silly. Experience tells me that whenever you can give the work room to evolve freely, it's a very good idea to do so. Onwards!

Hunter's Monologue

(Simple speech but charismatic. Like a taxi driver who's a natural-born storyteller.)

"I love the forest because it's simple. People are complicated, you know? You got smart people, stupid people, rich people, poor people, everybody wants something, and you don't know what it is. In the forest, everyone just wants one thing: to live.

"Except for the wolf. The wolf is different. He wants something, let me tell you. He wants something else.

"The lady at the inn said there wasn't any wolf. Right, so that's stupid because I've seen it with my own eyes, okay? I know the forest here better than anyone. But that's people for you, right? Everyone thinks they're smarter than everyone else. Like the innkeeper, her husband, right? I told him it's bad luck to eat meat on a Friday, and he laughs at me. So what do you think happens? A month later he gets bitten by a snake. Who's so smart now, eh? Not you, that's for sure. And not your lady too, who tells me there's no wolf even though I saw him with my own eyes, and then goes and sends her kid to the forest all by herself. Her lucky day, by the way. If I hadn't been there, she would have disappeared, like that hermit guy.

You know why I was there? I was looking for wolfie. I have an unfinished business with Mr. Wolf, and I'm going to finish it. And I knew he was around; the forest tells you those things, if you know how to listen. It's an intuition you get, a certain smell, weird little sounds.

"So I'm tracking him, and all of a sudden I hear something, this strange sound, never heard something like that in the forest. I thought at first it was a demon, but it turned out to be that girl from the inn. She had a strange voice, I think she was crying. She got lost.

"You wanna know something? I'll tell you right now. When I was talking to the girl, I heard something in the trees, right behind her. There was something there. Something big. I heard it moving away, and there's only one creature in that forest that moves like that. The inn lady says there's no wolf? Fine. I'm telling you if I had arrived a bit later, there would have been no girl either."

Writing the three monologues took about an hour. The personalities of the characters, which were kind of general and vague before, are now quite fascinating—at least to me. The girl is deliberately more generic (heroes usually are, because you need everyone to identify with them), but the hunter and the wolf are unique, and what's even better is that there's an interesting kind of relationship between them. Those two characters can hold a good story together.

I now feel I have the raw materials I need to start writing; the dry study stage is done. Next, we move on to wet studying.

> The lines between different elements of the process are often blurrier in practice than they are in theory. In this case, notice how some of the stuff I did for the dry exploration serves as wet exploration as well—especially the monologues and the description of the path.

The Wet Study

Wet studying is about doing some work you don't intend to use. You give yourself a bit of time to practice and experiment, without the anxiety of expectations.

To figure out where I should spend my *wet* studying efforts, the question I need to ask myself is: how do I feel about my ability to write this story with confidence and flow? What areas am I worried about? Where does my vision feel too vague? Is there a certain aspect of the work where I don't feel sure of my skills?

The truth is that I feel quite good about most of it—partly because the dry study included some wet studying as well. One thing I'm not so sure about is the writing style. I know I'm aiming for a good blend of exciting plot, light humor, and short, sensual descriptions, but that's a pretty general idea and not something specific I can imagine vividly.

The following paragraphs serve as writing rehearsals/experiments, focusing on that aspect.

1. A light, witty style, with storyteller talking directly to reader:

   It wasn't LRRH's fault that, less than an hour after promising Mom with complete conviction that she would not leave the path under any circumstances, she found herself in a lovely little lake deep in the forest. Let me tell you how this came to pass, and you will see for yourself that destiny itself was the culprit.

2. A more earnest style:

   As she passed through the old gate and left the village, an intoxicating sense of liberation swept over LRRH. She felt like a bird born in captivity, who suddenly found herself out of her cage. She was by herself in the great big world with no grown-up to make her do this or not do that; if she wished to leave the path, she could do that. It was her choice—and she chose to stay on the path. A big girl like herself should keep her promises!

3. Adding a touch of philosophizing:

LRRH passed the old gate, feeling solemn. It wasn't the first time she had passed through it, of course, but it was the first time she had done so without having to make sure no one was watching. It felt good.

She passed by the grove, in which her little makeshift lair was still hidden—unknown to any but herself. Why did the trees suddenly look so small and dreary?

As we grow older, yesterday's adventure becomes today's routine; what was once a dream, often turns into a chore. This is a fact of life, and LRRH was learning it now. The bushes—until yesterday, a forbidden place of danger and adventure—had somehow instantly turned into a bunch of boring old plants. A new and more exciting frontier was waiting for her to explore.

4. Trying an embellished version:

LRRH opened the old gate and ceremoniously passed through it. It was the first time she was going to the forest.

That's not quite true: it was the first time she's done so with permission. Without permission, she and her brother Edwin had been to the forest plenty of times.

That's also not quite true: what they had called "the forest" was really a bushy grove that lay between the village and the real forest. It was a wonderland of adventure and danger, full of brave heroes and hideous monsters. When an adult from the village would happen on the path, both hero and monster would crawl into "the cave"—a narrow space under the largest bush.

Now she herself was walking along the path like one of the adults. She felt the prickly chill of the cool air against her warm cheeks. The maple trees were still mostly green, but a faint autumn blush was already visible at the very edges of their leaves. Through the light fog of early morning, LRRH could see the massive trees of the forest itself:

heavy, dark, silent, the huge disciplined soldiers of mother nature. Her heart was beating fast. Yes, she was afraid—but it was not the ugly, incapacitating fear of something bad just about to happen. It was the energizing fear of something new; the kind of fear that announces an upcoming adventure.

* * *

None of this is great at all, but they give me what I want: a feel for the writing style I'm going for.

Experiment 4 is too description-heavy, but the tone is right: I like the juvenile point of view, combined with the use of nature to create mood and a light touch of deeper thought (e.g., the two kinds of fear). It feels like a good mix. I also love the lightness of 1. Number 3 is all wrong—but that is okay: that's what experiments are for! Oftentimes, beginning wrong will teach you more than being right will.

The most important result, however, is just that the project is no longer a foreign land to me, so to speak. I have visited it, and thus, I feel more confident going into it "for real."

The Premake

Having developed the plot, the characters, and the setting, and having determined the writing style I'm going for, I feel that my vision is now solid and exciting enough to carry a healthy production stage. The story is real, it exists in my mind; I know what it's going to be before I write a single word of it. Having gone through all the steps of the process with me, I hope you're at a similar place.

Now, it's time to create a premake that captures it all.

Let me share with you that, at this point, I'm so itching to start writing that I'm tempted to skip the premake altogether. The vision feels very solid and I have my concept outlined already;

doing another capture feels excessive. I'll do it anyway, of course: it only takes a few minutes, and I know intellectually (even if I don't feel that way right now) that it's important. That's just part of being a disciplined creative professional—and I trust this process.

The Premake

BACKGROUND: *Village, northern Europe before the 20th century, on the edge of an ancient forest. Rumors of a dangerous mythical man-wolf creature (not unlike the Yeti). LRRH—an imaginative, curious girl—believes the myth. Her mom, a practical woman and owner of local pub, does not. Mom sends LRRH to grandma's cottage deep in the forest.*

- *LRRH in forest. She's excited. She observes, listens, smells, touches. Animals, birds, insects. Forest more fascinating than path, but she keeps to it.*

- *Makes a mistake, goes on a smaller forking path. Realizes her mistake, but forest is much more interesting here. Go back? She thinks smaller path re-converges with main path. Continues.*

- *Spots big animal. Is this the wolf? Afraid but too curious to just leave.*

- *It's a boar. It scares her, stumbles off path, basket of food tumbles down slope. Climbs down to get it.*

- *Away from the path, forest is glorious. Lots of cute animals. Plays, loses track of time.*

- *Unknowingly scares away the wolf's prey. He's hungry and angry (we switch to his POV which is semi-human).*

- *LRRH notices something's wrong; animals fleeing. Mist thickens to fog; sun gone; cold. Forest suddenly ominous.*

- *Tries to get back to path but can't find the way. Wolf follows her. He finds her funny. Easy prey. She's like a sweet cookie to him.*

- *Just before wolf pounces, hunter arrives. Furious at finding LRRH alone in the forest. She tells him about grandma. The wolf overhears; decides to pay her a visit.*

Notes:

- The clipped and abbreviated writing is designed to help me skim through the premake very quickly—and often—during the Production stage. That's also the reason for using a bulleted list of story beats.

- In this description, I'm blending wet and dry thinking. I want the premake to contain both structure and flow.

- The beats are evenly developed; no beat stands out as being more or less detailed than the rest. This allows me and my reviewers to get an accurate preview of the piece.

- Short as it is, the premake is written in a way that gives the casual reader a good grasp of where this is going—without requiring too much presentation or clarification. This is great for getting some feedback.

- I have also included two images with the premake. I feel they complete the vision and make a great single-glance reminder.

How detailed is my vision at this point?

- Some of the moments are very vivid to me—I can see them clearly in my mind's eye, almost as if I'm watching a film. The scene in which she gets scared by the boar and falls off the path is one example.

- Other moments are more conceptual. The ending is one example: I know *what* is going to happen, but I can't really see it playing with the same kind of clarity. This is good enough for now, but I might have to go back for a brief wet/dry studying session before I attempt to write these parts.

- In terms of dialogue, perhaps one or two lines of dialogue are currently clear in my mind. All the rest is quite vague.

This is as good as it needs to get; I am finally ready to start writing. I print the Premake and stick it on the wall in front of me. Looking at it should never require more than a glance; if it takes more than that, it'll either slow me down and break my creative flow or (more likely) won't be looked at often enough.

Chapter 27

Stage III: Production

Something to Change

The first step of production is, of course, creating my "something to change" pass: an initial version of the story, simple and crude and full of errors, which I can begin to gradually push toward the vision.

I can use the premake as the first pass (providing, of course, that I save a copy somewhere so that I can return to it later). In this case, I decide not to do that: I have a fairly good grasp on what I'm going to write and how, and I want this first pass to flow freely from that vision, start to finish.
Here goes:

Pass 1

- LRRH leaves village; passes through grove leading to forest. Morning sun through light mist. Afraid. Exited. Adventure!

- Enters forest. Massive trees. Quiet. Birds. Rustling bushes— small animals. Fresh smell after night rain. Puddles. Wet leaves sparkling. Bird on path. LRRH starts enjoying herself.

- Two squirrels chasing each other. Butterflies. Huge butterfly flies into forest. Forest turns wilder, bigger. Darker.

- Path boring; forest fascinating. Little paths going into the growth—enticing her to explore. She fights the urge.

- Huge butterfly returns. Follows it. Doesn't notice she's taking a forking, smaller path. Easy mistake to make.

- Path narrows; slope on one side, cliff on the other side. Realizes her mistake. Before she can turn back, notices big shape ahead. Is it…the wolf? Glances back; the main path is right there. She can run to it. Curiosity takes over. She cautiously proceeds.

- It's a boar! Both startled. LRRH jerks back; stumbles off path, down slope. Basket rolls all the way down. She must fetch it. Climbs down.

- Hears stream. Suddenly very thirsty. Short hesitation. Decides to take a quick look.

- Reveal: Huge amazing butterflies, huge amazing tree, huge amazing mushrooms. Moss everywhere. LRRH awestruck.

- Switch to: not far, wolf preying upon doe and fawn. They are on their way to lake, to drink. Strong smells (also notices girl). Annoyed. Does not like people.

- Back to: LRRH playing with animals, feeding them, playing innkeeper with her guests. Squirrel leads her to little lake with cascade, small island, heron. Enchanted place. A fallen tree; LRRH walks over it, trying to get to small island. Then fawn and doe arrive. She's now overcome with excitement. She keeps quiet. Everything is super quiet.

- Loses her balance; SPLASH! Into the shallow water. Doe and fawn flee. She stumbles out of water, tries to find the deer, but can't find them.

- Tries to get back to lake but can't figure out her path. Cloud covers sun; everything turns grey. Wet, shivering. Something big is moving somewhere. She's afraid.

- A flock of birds suddenly take off at once, she screams, runs. Stumbles over grandma's basket; some of the food is gone. Tries to find path, but only gets more lost. Screams for help, but stops; obviously pointless.

- Wolf follows her. Amused. Sadistic. Girl smell is strong and sweet, like a fresh cookie. Prepares to pounce.

- Hunter appears out of nowhere; wolf stops mid-pounce. This makes a loud noise. Waits. Listens.

- Hunter heard the noise. Tries to see what it was. LRRH hugs him, face wet with tears. "What are you doing here?"— "mom sent me to grandma, she lives up the stream. Don't tell her I left the path, I didn't mean to… [blubbers on]."

- Wolf decides to get grandma; leaves quietly.

- Hunter still searching for whatever made the strange noise. Listening, sniffing. Finally, he finds something that tells him all. Says nothing to LRRH, except "come, I'll take you to your grandma." They leave, LRRH holding hunter's large hand. She feels safe.

* * *

This first pass took a little over an hour to write. I did very little editing while writing, although I did run into a few dead-ends and had to erase or change a previous sentence to get out of it. Nevertheless, for the most part, what you've just read is my stream of consciousness. This was only made possible because of the four-hour investment in developing a solid vision. I have so much raw material to work with that I was able to whip up a solution to any problem that presented itself.

For example, before writing the first pass, I didn't have a clear idea of how LRRH would scare off the deer. I did know, however, that there was a lake with a tree hanging over the water and that there was an island that you could get to by walking over the tree. This all came up in the dry study, just as a fun setting—I did not know at the time that it would end up having a function; but it presented an almost ready-made solution to that problem. In fact, it became the turning point of the entire scene: the moment she turns from dry and happy to wet and miserable is also the moment in which the forest turns from an enchanted wonderland to a grim and menacing place.

Notes:

- In capturing each story beat, I tried to balance wet and dry thinking: on the wet side, writing with free creative flow and using ideas as they came (e.g., when dialogue suggested itself), and on the dry side, using abbreviated writing and bullet points to keep the writing speedy and editable.

- In some cases, I had in mind the final sentence I was going to end up writing. I resisted the temptation to write it and instead wrote an abbreviated capture. This keeps the pass even and the process gradual and healthy. It also follows the principle of "keeping your mind ahead of the work."

- Notice how simple this first pass is. It's not trying to overreach or solve too many problems. It's just a slightly more elaborate version of what the premake already is.

- I feel more comfortable shaping the story in present tense, like a screenplay. I'll change it to past tense in a later pass.

First Pass Critique

It's time to stop writing and start reading. I take a break because it's hard for me to be objective right now. When I get back, I first glance through my premake, then I read the first pass a couple of times—once quickly, with an eye for big issues, and once more slowly, with an eye for smaller issues. I ask myself: "What few and specific improvements would advance my work the farthest toward my vision?"

Here are the answers from my inner critic, going from major to minor:

- We need to see the wolf's response to the prey escaping, as indicated in the premake. <<This important note is a direct result of comparing the pass with the premake; I would not have noticed that otherwise.

- The beginning should be slow, but not boring. <<This isn't a revision note, just something to keep in mind for the next pass—a perfectly legitimate and proactive note to give your inner artist.

- The first wolf scene feels too basic. Make the intro more exciting. He should feel disturbing and dangerous.

- The squirrel leading her to the lake is too cutesy. Find a different solution.

- In the "fall from grace" moment, have the log swing or break to symbolize that "the forest betrays her."

Second Pass

For the next pass, I can choose whether I want to only make these changes (simpler) or to try and incorporate them into a more general development pass. I choose the second option for two reasons: to avoid boring you with too many versions, and because I feel confident enough to do so (due to having a strong vision).

Pass 2

1. LRRH leaves village. Excited; never been deep in the forest before. She and her brother often play in the grove and imagine it's "the forest"; now it's the real thing. Goes past the grove. In the light mist, the slowly advancing forest feels sombre. She's slightly afraid, but also eager for the coming adventure.

2. Enters forest. Large trees, but not huge. Lots of tree stumps, trees not too dense, forest quite lit. Smell of fresh earth after rain. Trees are very tall. She feels small. All is rather quiet. Feels like a church. An occasional rustling noise at the path's edges, maybe small animals? She can't see any. Walks between the rain puddles. Small bird with red head hops on path. She is also a "red hood"…LRRH laughs at the thought, cheers up. Talks to the bird.

3. Two squirrels chasing each other, squeak and make a lot of noise, cross path and disappear up a tree. She tries to find them again, but can't. Yellow and white butterflies; she loves them. Imagines they're forest fairies. HA! Here's the king of butterflies, larger and very colorful. She tries to get closer to it but it keeps flying away. Finally flies into forest. She *really* wants to follow it in, but doesn't. She promised to stay on the path.

4. Continues to walk, now constantly trying to look as deep as she can into the forest. She's fascinated by what she can't see. The trees are now bigger and denser than before and green with moss. The forest is darker. Occasionally she catches a glimpse of a small animal that promptly scurries away. It's not that quiet anymore; or did her hearing get sharper? She feels the forest almost speaks to her.

5. Path now gets thinner. Climbs up along the side of a hill. On her right, quite a steep slope. Every so often, a very small path goes into the forest. Whose paths are these? Her imagination is in hyperdrive. Maybe they belong to the wild forest people. She fights the urge to try one of them, just for a little bit, just to see what's there.

6. She spots "the king of butterflies" on a rock. She tries again to get closer, again she fails. It flies along the path; she's focused on it, willing it to stay on the path. Slowly, she's getting closer. A loud CRACK snaps her out of it! She looks around, startled. The path is blurry and very narrow—is

it even a path at all? She realizes she had inadvertently turned into one of the "wild forest people" paths.

7. A large obscure shape is moving between the trees. That's where the noise came from. Is that…the wolf? She is at once afraid and excited. She glances back. The real path is just a few steps behind her, but she can't just go back; she has to know what this is. She advances cautiously.

8. LRRH steps on a twig, which snaps loudly; the shape lets out a weird noise; it's moving towards her…she takes a step back, and then…the shape turns out to be huge wild boar. Startled, she takes a few quiet steps back; stumbles on a rock, the ground disappears from under her feet; she finds herself sliding down the hill. She breaks the fall, but her basket rolls all the way down. What to do? If she comes back empty handed, mom will never trust her again. She can see the basket; it's just a few steps down.

9. The descent is harder than she expected. She needs to climb down, using her hands for balance, over logs and rocks. It takes a while to find a safe way down. Finally, she gets to the basket and collects The scattered food. She hears a stream somewhere nearby; realizes she's horribly thirsty. Hesitates, then decides: just a quick sip and she'll climb right up again.

10. Follows the sound a little further down. "King of butter-flies" makes another appearance. She turns a rock corner and suddenly, an amazing spectacle is revealed: a magnificent, massive tree covered with moss, branches so heavy the lower ones sit on the ground. Dozens of giant butterflies, even bigger and brighter than the one she was following. Under the tree is a small clear stream. Fingers of sunlight penetrate the leaves and mist to shed magical light on everything they touch. Small leaves tumble and sparkle, adding to the enchantment. LRRH climbs one of the low branches. A butterfly lands right on her forehead; it tickles!

11. Not far from the tree, a doe and her fawn walk along a narrow trail, flanked by a sheer drop of rock. About 10 yards above the trail, there's a flat plateau. On the plateau, a pair of yellow unblinking eyes. They are focused on the deer below. Hair surrounds the eyes; below the eyes is a nose. The nose sniffs the air. The nose twitches in surprise; he looks around. There's a human in the forest. An unfamiliar human. He doesn't like humans; they're nothing but trouble. Tasty, but troublesome.

12. Focus snaps back to deer. He's very hungry. If he attacks now, he'll probably get the fawn but not the doe. He waits; the trail to the lake, which is where they're going, passes between two rocks. Once they get there, he'll be able to get both. Patience! He imagines the chase, the pounce, the sinking of teeth in flesh. He salivates and drools. Just a few more minutes…he advances, quiet as a shadow, along the cliff.

13. LRRH, meanwhile, is trying to seduce a squirrel to take a bite of grandma's bread. A second squirrel joins in. She imagines herself as innkeeper, with squirrels as guests. Squirrels take off; where did they go? She follows in the general direction and discovers a tiny lake that the little stream cascades into. The water is super clear; you can see some fishes swimming about. In the middle of the lake is a small island. A few ducks and a beautiful big heron stand on the island. A fallen tree creates a bridge leading straight to it. She cannot resist: she decides to cross over.

14. The wolf is poised above the dead-end passage to the lake. The deer are nearly there; just a few yards left! Suddenly… he spots the wretched human girl. She's walking over a log, carefully balancing herself. She'll ruin everything… He curses quietly. Out of the corner of his eye, he sees the doe stop right in front of the dead-end gap. She sniffs the air and continues. The wolf is about to pounce!

15. Just then, LRRH sees the deer. An involuntary spasm of surprise and delight. The tree shifts and she loses balance,

screams, and falls right into the water with a huge splash! The doe and fawn turn tail and run; the wolf almost gives chase, but realizes he will not catch them. They are gone. He is furious beyond words. The girl will pay for this. If he can't eat a fawn, he'll eat a human child instead.

16. LRRH stumbles out of the water, runs after the deer. She's sorry she scared them, but she's even sorrier she missed them; they were so pretty! She can't find them. She listens: all is very quiet. They're gone. Then she senses—a kind of a primal sense—something big moving right above her and a flock of birds take off at once, making a huge racket. She screams; she runs—a panicked, aimless run. She stumbles over something. Gets up. It's the basket. She picks it up, not realizing how much lighter it is. Where is she? The lake is gone. The tree is gone. She's wet. She's shivering. She's utterly lost. She screams for help, but the scream is absorbed in the vast space of the forest. It's pointless.

17. Wolf follows her. Why hasn't he attack yet? He's not sure. He's amused. He's also a bit curious. The food from the basket calmed him down a bit. Humans are very strange. He continues to follow very silently. Every now and again, he deliberately breaks a twig to keep her scared. Somehow the fear makes her smell even sweeter. Well, that was entertaining, but the hunger is back. Time to finish this. He prepares… and *pounces.*

18. At that precise moment, a strong an unexpected noise surprises the wolf, causing him to halt mid-pounce. Out of nowhere, a large human emerges. The halted pounce was noisy; the big man heard it. The wolf waits, weighing his options. Listens.

19. The child is terrified for a second, but then she hugs the big man. She calls him "Will." He is not happy. Asks her what she's doing there. She tells him, crying and sniffling, "Mom sent me to grandma, she lives upstream. Don't tell her I left the path, I didn't mean to…" [she blubbers on, telling her story so confusedly that it cannot be followed].

20. The wolf is frozen in place, eyes boring into the humans. He's enraged. For the second time in less than an hour, he was denied his prey at the very last moment. But he thinks, too. There's a grandma up the stream. He hasn't been there in a long while. And the child is on her way. And he's very hungry. Well, if he can't have a doe and a fawn, he'll have a human woman and a human child. It's only fair. He turns and sneaks away.

21. The hunter's ears perk up. He walks towards where he knows he heard something that does not belong in this forest. He searches. He sniffs. He notices the trampled undergrowth. He sees the marks of the wolf's claw, where he used a branch to halt his pounce. He stares at it for a long time. LRRH asks what's there. "Nothing. Come, I'll take you to your grandma." They hold hands. LRRH feels happy and safe again.

> Pass 1 was written from scratch; pass 2 and all subsequent passes are iterations done on the existing text.

This pass took about two hours—again without much editing, but with plenty of pausing and imagining different scenarios. The typing itself took about only a quarter of that time; the rest was work done inside my head.

Critique and Chunking

With the second pass done, I stop working and call in my critic again. I also show it to a friend for feedback, since the story beats are quite well established at this point.

Here's the "shopping list" combining all the notes, from the major to the minor:

- The forest is too busy with magical elements; take some out.

- Make sure it's clear that the wolf in the story is a man-wolf.

- It's hard to buy that she would think of the deer after falling into the cold water. Look for an alternate solution.

- Make beat 10 a bit longer. <<When possible, number or label the elements in your passes. It makes it easier to critique.

- Use specific names of plants and trees in the descriptions (but only those that a girl might know). It adds believability.

Before I continue to pass 3, there is an important thing I need to consider.

Pass 1 took about an hour; pass 2 took about two hours; pass 3 would probably take much longer—possibly a whole day. That's way too long for a single pass; as we know, a healthy process is made of short, simple, and focused passes. Also, I expect the final piece to be about 15–20 pages long, which is too large for working in simple passes. So, I need to *slice* the piece to subprojects and focus on each slice in turn.

The process is identical for each slice; so, for the purpose of this demonstration, we'll only do the very last slice—points 17 to 21: the attack.

The Attack

As we've seen in Section 6, a subproject like this could include the entire process with all its elements. Here, I don't need the Concept stage, since I already know what I'm working toward. I do need to do some more studying though, since I feel my vision for this area is not as developed as I'd like it to be.

I won't go into the details of developing the Vision for this subproject, since it's identical to the process already demonstrated. Basically, I dry-studied the geography of the area in which the wolf attacks the girl, came up with some setting elements to help establish the mood, and wet-studied possible dialogues and thoughts for the different characters. Once I felt my vision for this slice of the story was solid, I created a separate premake to capture it.

The full process of writing this section of the story ended up taking more than 20 passes and involved even more slicing down the road. I will summarize it using the three major phases of the Production process: *blocking, shaping,* and *refining.* Just keep in mind that these are not three passes, but three *groups* of passes.

One last note: to simplify the presentation, and since I believe the principle of separating critic and artist is understood by now, I marked the critic's major notes on the text itself.

Blocking

In the blockings phase, I'm laying down the "skeleton" of the story—the bare sequence of events. This took just a few quick passes to complete. As you'll see, it's still formatted as a bulleted list (a dry set of wet captures), but it's a more detailed version than what we had in the second pass (paragraphs 17–21):

- Wolf follows LRRH. Laughs at her awkward human way of moving.

- Breaks branch, scares her on purpose. Enjoys seeing her fear. Makes her smell even sweeter. Cannot resist any longer; he's going to attack. << This has a deeply disturbing undertone, but I think that's good. Even though you know where the story is going (it is Little Red Riding Hood after all), you can't help being afraid for her. It's very sinister.

- There's only one route she can take; wolf does his "slow parkour" thing. Ends up lurking in a bush by the path.

- Could run and catch her but where's the beauty in that?

- LRRH arrives at the spot, as planned. He pounces.

- Stops mid pounce—something is off, he saw a big shape moving.

- It's a man. The girl screams but then seems to recognize him. << Add: wolf notices weapon—this is why he doesn't attack.

- Hunter looks around. Stares at bush but can't see wolf.

- Girl explains what she's doing in the forest. Mentions grandma and where she lives.

- Wolf furious: lost his prey at the very last moment—for the second time! Feels like attacking but decides to get grandma and wait for LRRH to get there. He leaves.

- Hunter notices a movement; examines the bush. Trampled undergrowth, and the smoking gun: a claw mark (made when wolf stopped mid-pounce). Stares at it.

- LRRH asks what's there. Turns away saying, "Nothing. Come, I'll take you to your grandma. Your mother may think otherwise, but the forest is not a place for little girls."

Shaping

Here, I'm starting to put some flesh on the story's bare bones. This is more of a wet phase: the bullets are gone, and juicy details start to emerge. It took five or six passes to complete—mainly pushing mood and emotional tone and making sure everything makes sense.

(Need to switch everything to past tense)

The wolf puts his paw on branch; gently presses. Looks at girl. She climbs. Smiles an ugly smile. Humans are weird. They have no refinement. She doesn't stop to sniff, listen, observe. Just trumps forward making a big noise. Only humans do that.

Increases pressure on branch. SNAP! Branch breaks loudly. LRRH jumps, scared. Small scream. Slides and falls. Looks up. Wide blue eyes looking frantically around. "Anyone there…?"

Wolf looks. Her knee is now bleeding a bit. He's salivating again. He's so hungry but the game is so enticing. Her fear is so tangible, he can almost touch it. It smells sweet. He won't be able to hold it much longer.

Wolf slides down onto tree, climbs down to low branch, drops into bushes. Yes, he could just run after her and catch her easy, but he likes a precise conclusive attack. More satisfying. A chase is an attack that failed.

From behind a tree, she comes into view. He prepares for the pounce. A few more steps… [add countdown]

He pounces.

A fraction of a second before the pounce, he catches a glimpse of something big moving behind the girl. He stops mid jump, drops back into the bush. Suffers a painful whiplash. [add claw mark, to connect nicely with last beat].

The big shape turns out to be a man. The girl screams. He covers her mouth with a big hand. "It's me. Will." Wolf notices he's armed. [recognizes him from last time; doesn't want to clash with him again].

Hunter looks around. Stares at bush but can't see wolf. [move this to after next paragraph?]

The wolf is frozen in place, eyes boring into the two humans with red hot fury. For the second time in less than an hour, his prey was snatched away at the very last moment. He forces himself to calm down and think, listen, and wait. A predator needs patience.

The girl hugs the hunter, tears streaming freely down her cheeks. The hunter seems angry. "What are you doing here, little girl? "Mom sent me to grandma, she lives upstream. Don't tell her I left the path, I didn't mean to…I was trying to keep to the path but then the kind of butterfly confused me and there was a boar in the forest people's path and then I fell and wanted to drink and I found this tree, and then I fell into the lake and couldn't find the way back—" [break this down—a conversation not a monologue]

Wolf smiles his ugly smile. So, there's a grandma up the stream… he hasn't been there for a long while. He's still furious, but now he knows where the girl is heading. He will get there faster. If he can't have a doe and a fawn, he'll have a grandma and a granddaughter instead. It's only fair.

He turns and sneaks away.

The hunter's ears prick up. He signals "quiet" to LRRH. Stares at the bush again. Did he see something move?

LRRH is asking questions, but he doesn't answer. Moves towards the bush where he saw the movement. Pulls out a long knife. He reaches the bush. Searches. Sniffs. Pushes the branches aside. Nothing there. Notices the trampled undergrowth. Then his gaze falls on the deep mark made by the wolf's claws when he stopped mid-pounce. He stares at it for a long time. LRRH asks what's there.

"Nothing. Come, I'll take you to your grandma." Holds her hand. "Your mother may think otherwise, but the forest is not a place for little girls."

Refining

This is the final step in our case study journey. The content is already there, with the structure and most of the details in place. What remains to be added is beauty and craftsmanship: style, language, changing from present tense (screenplay-style) to past tense (storybook-style), refining dialogues, etc. It took 10–15 passes to complete, which is very much in alignment with the exponential progress graph from Section V.

The Attack—Final Text

The Wolf put his hairy paw on the branch and pressed it down gently. He watched the red hood moving slowly through the fog, like a stain of blood floating in murky waters. A boulder was blocking her way and she was trying to climb over it. Her movements were awkward, inefficient, pathetic. The Wolf smiled an ugly smile. Humans were strange. They had no refinement. He had been following her for a while now, and in all that time, not once did she stop to sniff, listen, or observe. She just kept moving forward, graceless, noisy, panting, trampling. Only humans walked this way.

He increased the pressure on the branch. CRACK! It snapped loudly. The girl jumped up like a scared rabbit, gave a little yelp, slipped on the sloping rock face and fell. She lifted her head, her big blue eyes darting frantically around.

"Hello? Anyone there?"

The Wolf snickered quietly to himself. It had been years since he'd had that much fun. Humans were not his usual dish; they were tasty, but much more trouble than they were worth. Years ago, he had devoured a kid and was forced to hide for weeks as a result. An entire armed village came looking for him. Eventually he had to leave that area. That was because they found the kid's remains. Of this girl, he promised himself smacking his lips, there will be no remains. They'll think she just got lost in the woods. It happens.

The girl got up, rubbing her knee. She was bleeding now. Just a little, but enough to make his mouth water. He was hungry, very hungry. He would have to finish it soon. Her fear was palpable, he could almost touch it. It smelled sweet.

He could see clearly where she was heading. There was only one route she could take up the hill. He slipped off, skipped easily up the rock formation, reached a tree overhanging the path, and climbed it nimbly. There, he waited until the red spot once again emerged through the fog. He slid along a branch, dropped down and landed noiselessly in the bushes at the edge of the path.

He knew he could just chase her and catch her; that would be easy. But he liked the cleanliness and elegance of a precision attack: one jump, one slash, and that was it. A chase was the sign of a failed attack. To him, accuracy was part of the challenge of hunting.

He heard her footsteps approaching. His muscles tensed; he became a steel trap. He could see her through the branches. Three steps away. Two steps. One step.

He pounced.

He caught sight of a large and heavy shape moving quickly forward, right behind the girl. He managed to stop himself mid-pounce, his claws boring deep into the tree trunk, fighting the immense thrust of his body. He landed heavily in the bushes again, his arms aching from the sudden and unexpected effort. He suffered a painful lash from a released branch, adding a nasty cut to his cheek. He wanted to breathe heavily, but forced himself to take slow, long, quiet breaths instead. He looked up and peered through the branches.

From among the pine trees behind the girl emerged a large man dressed in dark green. A sharp glimmer told the Wolf he was carrying a metal blade. The girl tried to scream, but the big man quickly put a massive hand over her mouth and silenced her. "It's just me," he said. His voice was gruff.

The Wolf sat frozen, his eyes boring into the two humans, his blood boiling with fury. For the second time in less than an hour, his prey was snatched away at the very last moment. He considered lashing out at them, attacking both, letting his rage take over; but he had recognized the man, saw his blade, and knew it would not be a good idea. No, he was going to be smart. He was going to wait. A moment of distraction, and he'd be able to grab the girl and run. Patience and self-discipline are a predator's best friends.

The man looked around anxiously. For a moment, he was staring directly at the Wolf; but the bushes were dense and the wolf was still. The man could not see him. He continued to scan the environment, slowly, meticulously, the blade still drawn and ready.

The girl was sobbing hard now. The man released her. His hand was wet with her tears; distractedly, he wiped it on his shirt. She hugged him.

"Oh I'm so glad you found me Mr. Jacob!" she sniffled. "I was so afraid… I mean, not really afraid," she stopped sobbing and quickly wiped her face. "Only a little, because I couldn't find the path."

The hunter looked at her with both astonishment and exasperation. "What are you doing here, kid?"

"I—mom sent me here. Not exactly here I mean, just to the forest—"

"Your mom sent you to the forest?" His face grew incredulous. "Alone?"

"To bring grandma her food," she showed him the basket. "She lives up the stream, right after an old bridge, and we send her food you know, but Maria was sick today and Mom said I could go, and then I saw a boar at the forest people's trail…"

"The forest people?" Mumbled the hunter.

The Wolf smiled his ugly smile again. So, there's a grandma living alone beyond the old bridge, is there? He hadn't been there in a long while. Very interesting indeed. He was still furious, but now he had a plan. If he couldn't have a doe and a fawn, he'd have a human grandma and a human granddaughter instead. It was only fair.

Quietly, carefully, he snuck away through the undergrowth.

"...And then I fell into the lake, and the animals disappeared, and I tried to find the way back to the path—"
She fell instantly quiet as the hunter suddenly stiffened and stared. He lifted the knife again. Did he just see a shadow shift? Did the shadow have big yellow eyes...?
He kept staring. Nothing was moving now.

"What is it?" Whispered the girl.

He didn't answer. He moved slowly forward, then stopped, listened, and sniffed. Was he imagining it, or was it really that familiar foul scent? He pushed the bush's branches aside. Nothing there now. Nothing but the lingering scent, trampled earth and a broken branch. His gaze fell on the tree trunk.

"What is it?" Asked the girl again.

Imprinted in the wood, a few inches from his face, was the deep, sharp, and very fresh mark of a claw.

"Nothing," said the hunter. He turned to her and held her hand. "Come on, I'll take you to grandma. Your mom may think otherwise, but the forest is not a safe place for little girls."

Conclusion

This concludes my demonstration of the creative workflow. I hope you enjoyed it and that it made the principles discussed in this book feel more concrete.

Let me emphasize here that I am not a professional fiction writer. In fact, I'm not even an amateur one. I therefore expect that some literary aspects of this work that have nothing to do with the process, such as vocabulary or writing style, may not be up to the standards of professional writers. Nevertheless, I do believe that this case study demonstrates not only the process itself, but also that a person who understands the principles of the creative workflow can achieve reasonable results even in an area he/she is far from practiced in.

Whatever your own creative interests are or will be in years to come, I hope you'll find these same principles helpful in achieving a fun, confident, and stress-free workflow.

AT A GLANCE:

THE WORKFLOW

From blank page
to the refined piece

1. CONSIDER CONTEXT
WHAT'S THE PURPOSE YOUR WORK IS GOING TO SERVE?

2. COME UP WITH A CONCEPT
BUILD AN EXCITING CORE IDEA FROM A PILE OF 'BAD' IDEAS.

3. DEVELOP YOUR CREATIVE VISION
DEVELOP A DETAILED MENTAL PREVIEW OF YOU WORK,
THEN **CAPTURE** IT AS A PREMAKE.

4. PRODUCE YOUR WORK
START WITH "SOMETHING TO CHANGE",
AND GRADUALLY IMPROVE IT TOWARDS YOUR VISION.

IF AT ANY POINT YOU FEEL CONFUSED OR OVERWHELMED...

- STOP WORKING, AND APPLY PATTERN-BREAKING TECHNIQUES
- TAKE A STEP BACK AND CONSIDER THE CONTEXT
- REVIEW THE PREMAKE AND RECONSTRUCT YOUR VISION
- CHUNK YOUR WORK TO TASKS/SUB-PROJECTS
- WRITE DOWN A SIMPLE SCHEUDLE
- RELAX AND TRUST THE PROCESS!

Section VIII

THE PRINCIPLES

A Deeper Look at the
Fundamentals of the
Creative Workflow

"Art is messy, art is chaos - so you need a system."

Andrew Stanton

Chapter 28

Key Concepts

Now that we've discussed the five elements of the creative work-flow in detail and have seen a complete case study, it's time to take a step back and have another look at the process as a whole. I believe that the key to understanding how something works, is understanding its basic design principles. So in this last chapter, I'd like to highlight a few key concepts that stand as the backbone of the workflow approach.

Structured Chaos

Flow and structure are two opposing and necessary components of both the creative process and the artwork it produces. Structure brings clarity and control, while flow brings emotional connection and creative zest. The workflow we've discussed strives to balance those two forces and to create synergy between them. This is achieved by:

- Learning when and how to use *dry and wet thinking* at the capture level, which is the basic building block of creativity

- Balancing wet and dry thinking throughout the process: *wet/dry studies*, *wet/dry critiquing*, and layering *wet/dry passes*.

- Providing a system that creates "structured chaos"—a planned and controlled set of free-flowing creative bursts.

Short Bursts

Chunking your work down to short bursts, each lasting between a few minutes and a couple of hours, keeps you both focused and effective. The following tools support that idea:

- The *capture* as the basic building block of the workflow. Each capture is a short and hyperfocused burst of creative force.

- *Working in passes* as a way of chunking down the long Production process into short captures, each aiming to improve the work in a specific and simple way.

- *Adaptive planning* as a way of putting the above ideas into practice, providing both control and flexibility in planning your short bursts.

Big Picture

In my lectures, I often use the metaphor of an ant walking on a human body. To that ant, every minor zit and scratch looks like a striking imperfection; however, it will not be able to tell that the person is missing an arm. In the same way, creatives look so closely at their work that they often see it's bumps and scratches more clearly than they see more serious problems.

The following tools were introduced to deal with that challenge:

- The *premake* works together with the concept of *working in passes*—the former providing you with a steady destination, and the latter equipping you with a reliable method of getting there without losing focus.

- *Chunking to layers* helps you break down the work to simpler parts without narrowing your focus.

- *Chunking to slices* works together with the tools of *context*, allowing you to narrow your area of focus while maintaining a strong connection with the bigger picture.

Accepting Mistakes

Fear of failure is, unfortunately, a self-fulfilling prophecy. Like a black hole, once you get sucked into the vortex, it gets increasingly hard to break away. In the words of Franklin D. Roosevelt: "the only thing we have to fear is fear itself."

Every stage of the workflow you've learned is designed to reduce fear, by adopting uncertainty and mistakes as a legitimate (and even necessary) part of the process:

- In the Concept stage, you build good concepts out of bad or silly ideas.

- In the Vision stage, *wet studies* allow you to make mistakes "off stage," without anxiety or consequences.

- In the Production stage, you start with a deliberately imprecise capture. Then, in each pass, mistakes and uncertainty are allowed and even expected, as you focus on *improvement* rather than *perfection*.

Fractals and Self-Similarity

Self-similarity allows you to use a small set of methods to control projects of many different types and sizes. It also allows you to be simple and complex at the same time—a quality valuable for both the process and the resulting artwork.

The book introduces self-similarity in the following areas:

- **Capturing.** Captures are repeated in different scales throughout the workflow. A capture's scale is independent of the scale of the idea it represents: a multi-million dollar project can be captured in a napkin doodle.

- **Chunking and subprojects.** In larger projects, the same Concept–Vision–Production workflow repeats itself in different scales.

- **The workflow is a standalone skill.** The set of methods described in this book can be applied across many creative mediums and disciplines.

Quality Boosts

The main purpose of this book has been to help you improve your workflow and your confidence as a creator. However, as creatives, what we care about the most at the end of the day is the quality of the artwork our workflow produces.

Here are some of the positive effects the workflow described in this book is going to have on your final work.

Originality. The workflow provides you with a dependable system of coming up with concepts that are based on a combination of happy accidents, associative connections, and most importantly, your unique personal point of view. Originality and freshness are supported not only in the Concept stage but also in the Vision and Production stages, by allowing chaos to co-exist with structure.

Flow. Great artwork often has a certain "flow" to it. It feels deceptively easy, as if it came out effortlessly, without a process involved. Ironically, it is precisely the process that creates that charming quality: the playfulness of the Concept stage, the familiarity acquired through the Vision stage, and the gradual growth in the Production stage. The balance of dry and wet capturing, which allows your work to connect equally with both parts of your audience's brain, also plays an important part.

Conceptual Clarity. Conceptual clarity is about conveying a strong and consistent concept to your audience. This is supported in each individual stage: you start by setting a clear destination (*concept*); you then expand that concept and anchor it (*vision* and *premake*); then you create the work while constantly referring to that anchor (*working in passes*).

In larger projects, the principle of *working in context* helps you make sure that every single element of the work follows and supports that clear concept.

Structural Clarity. Structural clarity is about conveying your clear concept in a way that's easy for your audience to follow. This is supported with various tools: chunking, dry captures, and working in passes.

Highly Polished Work. Doing detailed work with a high level of precision and rich texture is one of the greatest aspirations of every ambitious creative. The workflow provides several tools to facilitate that level of refinement: *dry studying* to supply you with an abundance of raw material to use, *working in passes* to help you deal with any level of details without losing control, and *chunking* to help you avoid feeling overwhelmed. In addition, time saved through improved effectivity (*hyperfocus* and *micro-deadlines*) can be used for additional refinement passes.

A Good Day's Work

In the introduction to this book, I made a few big claims about what you can expect from improving your workflow. Now that you have all the details, the overview, and the conceptual underlying principles of the workflow, I hope you feel that these claims were justified and that the promises were indeed made good on.

Above all, I hope I've been able to convince you of the two fundamental axioms that stand at the base of this book: (1) that having a robust and well-defined workflow is critical to your success, and (2) that the workflow can be learned and practiced as a standalone skill, that can be used in any creative project, in any medium, of any size or level of complexity.

If have convinced you of nothing else in this book except for these two points, I would still regard it as a good day's work.

Afterword

We're done!

This was quite a journey. We went through an extensive analysis of the creative workflow; so extensive, in fact, that you might be a bit overwhelmed right now. You may even find yourself intimidated by the whole thing: "Wait, what was it about the…Am I supposed to do a wet capture now? Dry capture? Or was it both? Wasn't there something about three phases of production? I can't remember anything!"

This is a danger I've been acutely aware of throughout the process of writing this book, and you should be aware of it too. Learning new techniques can create fear; I've seen it happen to students, and indeed, I've seen it happen to me. Fighting the fear of failure is one of the main goals of this book, and it would be unfortunate if it ended up *creating* that fear.

Here are three points to keep in mind if and when you do feel confused or intimidated by the workflow you've learned.

1. **Walking lessons.** The creative process is one of those things that are complicated to explain but easy to do. Like walking, for example: have you ever tried to explain to someone the mechanics of how you walk? As an animation teacher, I have given many such "walking lessons." It usually takes me four hours to explain just the *basics* of what the human body does when you walk in a straight line—never mind anything more complex than that. And yet when we walk, we just do it—it's not hard at all!

The creative workflow is just like that. It sounds complex when analyzed and explained, but once you've done it for a while, it becomes second nature—and you don't have to think about it as much.

2. **Make it your own.** The process I've described is not a formula. It's not a thing you just take as is, perform the designated actions in the correct order, and get the results. Rather, it's more of a recipe: it gives you a tried-and-tested *version* of the dish—but personal taste, common sense, available tools and ingredients, and a whole range of other factors could and *should* be taken into account as well. When it comes down to it, no two chefs will make a recipe exactly the same way.

Similarly, your personality and taste, the specifics of the project, and your creative medium will all influence your process. Experiment with the different tools, concepts, and tips you've learned, see what works for you and what doesn't; and feel free to change and adjust things to suit your needs. If you need to simplify some of the parts, do that; if you feel like something's missing, try to develop your own process tools. The most important thing to keep in mind is that the workflow is an important part of success. The rest is up for grabs.

3. **The process of the process.** Finally, the quest for a great creative process is *also* a process. Just like with working in passes, it's not really about *fixing* it but about gradual and constant

improvement. I still make plenty of workflow mistakes, and so will you; what's new is that you're now able to notice those mistakes faster and that you have a whole set of tools to help you course-correct.

To that point, I'd like to finish with the story of Sharon (not her real name), a talented interior designer to whom I showed one of the early drafts of this book. A few months later, she landed an exciting new job designing exhibition booths. This was a big opportunity for her, but her first stab at it was quite painful. "I made all the process mistakes you mention in your book," she complained. "I did it exactly wrong."

Oddly enough, that made me proud of both her and the book. I realized that she was now so aware of the importance of the workflow to the success of her work that when things went wrong, she immediately thought of *that* as the main cause of her trouble and was able to identify her process mistakes. Had she not read the book, she might have thought, "I'm not good at this," "I'm not talented enough," "I don't know enough about it." She could have lost the entire project over this, or she might have decided to take an expensive evening course to boost her "insufficient" skills. Meanwhile, her work would have continued under a heavy shadow of self-doubt and fear of failure.

Reading the book and understanding the power of the process prevented all this and sent her looking for what was really amiss: *not* her talent, *not* her knowledge or experience, but her creative *workflow*. As painful as the experience was for her, she learned something from it and came out stronger, producing much better results the next time around.

I find it beautiful that the ideas in this book helped Sharon, even though she completely failed to implement them. If that's the kind of insight and encouragement you can get out of *failing* to implement the workflow, just imagine what *succeeding* can do for you.

Final Thought...

I'd like to leave you with this final thought.

If you forget everything else you've read in this book, remember this: *follow the process*. Don't expect or demand immediate success. When you accept mistakes, imperfection, and searching as natural and necessary components of the process, you can relax and create with confidence and flow. I think you'll find that very often, that's all you really need in order to succeed.

Glossary

Blocking–Shaping–Refining: Three phases of the production stage. *Blocking* is laying down the main points of the work, *Shaping* is creating the bulk of the content, and *Refining* is adding and tweaking details and texture.

Capturing: Conveying the essence of a subject clearly and briefly.

Chunking: Dividing your work to logical segments and attaching a timeframe to each segment.

Chunking to layers: Chunking a project to subprojects to be worked on in chronological order. Typically, each layer focuses on a different aspect of the work.

Chunking to slices: Chunking a project to parallel subprojects in a way that doesn't require working in a specific order. All slices are typically focused on the same aspect of the work.

Concept: A viable solution to your creative challenge; a seed you can develop your work from.

Context: The larger project, or cause, that your work is a part of.

Creative vision: A mental preview of your final work.

Dry capture: Simplifying a subject through its structure; the subject as the sum of its parts. Ask yourself: how do I understand this? What is it made of?

Dry study: Gaining familiarity with your subject matter through researching and collecting (or inventing) information.

Even state: A state in which all the elements of the work are refined to the same extent.

Explosive progress: The typical nonlinear shape of working in passes. The work improves very quickly in the first few passes and slowly in later passes.

Fractal chunking: Chunking your work to subprojects, then creating each one with the same workflow of the larger work.

Idea: Any scrap of thought you come up with as you think creatively about your subject.

Layering/Clustering/Blending: Three ways of achieving wet/dry synergy in your work: *Layering* is alternating between wet/dry passes, *Clustering* is using a dry set of wet captures (see "Structured Chaos"), and *Blending* is using both approaches at the same time.

Linear chunking: Chunking your work to a simple string of tasks, to be performed one after the other (e.g., the Concept–Vision–Production sequence and the working in passes workflow). This kind of chunking works well for relatively short and simple projects, done by a single person.

Micro-deadline: Challenging yourself to finish a simple task in a short amount of time (usually no longer than two hours and mostly a lot less).

A pass: A segment of the production stage, designed to bring the entire work one simple step closer to the vision.

Placeholders: A capture fitted into a larger capture (typically the premake). Placeholders are widely used in creative mediums in which the final work is an arrangement of individual elements.

Premake: A capture that represents the vision, focusing and anchoring it for future reference. This is the heart and soul of the workflow: it's the apex of the preparation part and the reference point for the production part.

Structured chaos: An orderly and logical structure of messy, chaotic bursts. This is one of the underlying principles of the creative workflow, and it supports the balance of dry/ wet thinking.

Thinking patterns: A fixated or repetitive path of thinking that makes it hard to see things differently.

Wet capture: Simplifying a subject through its holistic nature. Ask yourself: how do I feel about this? What does it remind me of?

Wet study: Gaining familiarity with your subject matter through practicing it, and through experimenting with different options.

Working in passes: The process of starting with a rough approximation of the vision and then gradually getting it closer to the vision using a series of simple passes.

Zoom level: The level of detail you're focused on in a given moment.

Index